Lots of Laughter
Praise for the Good Old Days

"Remember now thy creator, in the days of thy youth."
Ecclesiastes 12:1

By
Valerie Knowles Combie

World rights reserved. This book or any portion thereof may not be copied or reproduced in any form or manner whatever, except as provided by law, without the written permission of the publisher, except by a reviewer who may quote brief passages in a review.

The author assumes full responsibility for the accuracy of all facts and quotations as cited in this book. The opinions expressed in this book are the author's personal views and interpretations and do not necessarily reflect those of the publisher.

Copyright © 2013 Aspect Books
ISBN-13: 978-1-4796-0189-9 (Paperback)
ISBN-13: 978-1-4796-0190-5 (ePub)
ISBN-13: 978-1-4796-0191-2 (Kindle/Mobi)

Library of Congress Control Number: 2013910944

Published by

www.ASPECTBooks.com

Contents

1. The Early Years in Cedar Grove 5
2. Those Busy Fun-Filled Days 10
3. Long Live the Apprenticeship System! 14
4. Of Manners and Behaviors 20
5. Religion Permeated Our Lives 26
6. Education, My First Love 32
7. The Domestic Front 37
8. A Ride Anyone? 42
9. Local Fruits 46
10. The Sea All Around Us 50
11. Indoctrination of Moral Principles 55
12. Communal Activities and Student Bonding 60
13. Security and Stability 63
14. Typical Caribbean Furniture 67
15. Other Activities 75
16. Social Traditions 79
17. Burial of the Dead 81
18. Other Eccentricities 83
19. Methods of Discipline 87
20. Migration 91

21. Of Senior Care and Other Considerations 96
22. Attractions and Entertainment 99
23. Of Parties and Such 102
24. Those Glorious Days 105
25. Some Popular Family Recipes 107
Glossary of Terms 110

Chapter 1

The Early Years in Cedar Grove

I could not wait for the morning to break. I was wide awake, but the alarm had not gone off. I must have had enough sleep. A searching glance at the luminous hands on the clock indicated that it was 2:30 a.m. I made a quick calculation and realized I had slept for six hours. Was that enough? Didn't I need seven or maybe eight hours of sleep? But I was wide awake, fully refreshed. Why waste precious time? I turned off the alarm, which had been set for 3:30 a.m., got out of bed, quietly walked to the bathroom, my sanctuary, closed the door, and then turned on the light so that the instant glare would not arouse my sleeping husband. For the next hour, I studied my Sabbath School lesson, read my Bible, and then studied the day's sections from the three devotional books I read daily. My devotional time each day reconnects me with God and helps me organize my activities for the day.

If it's Sunday, I will begin the laundry that had been sorted the night before. After completing the laundry, I telephone my friend, whom I will meet at 5:30 a.m. to walk "The Beast"—the long, steep, winding hill that leads from Scenic Drive to the Carambola Road in St. Croix. It's a challenging hike, but we enjoy the sheer pleasure that leads to exhaustion. After the two-hour walk I return home where I clean up, have breakfast, and then visit the hair dresser to get my weekly wash. After that, I return home and prepare lunch, which I often eat alone. Then I will iron and organize my clothes for the week, grade student papers to be returned the following day, or relax in front of the TV watching a comedy or a classic movie. I may pick fruits from the garden, or I may bake and make a Caribbean fruit punch. Later, I will watch *60 Minutes* to end my day. By 8:30 p.m., I will be in bed, having packed my bags for the following morning.

That is only one day, but the pattern is repeated daily, with Sabbath being the only exception. On the Sabbath, I sleep later, not having turned on the alarm the previous night, luxuriating in God's rest and my body's well-earned rest.

Every day I'm always occupied working in the garden, cleaning the house, reading, writing, or cooking. Many times I will listen to the radio or watch the television while I'm doing those things. I seldom do one thing only. The multitasker that I am requires me to have more than one iron in the fire. I always have something to do, and if I don't, I read or write. I have not experienced boredom. I don't know what it means to be bored because I am always occupied. It seems as if I never have enough time in the day to complete the many tasks and projects I would like to undertake, but God knows why He has given us only twenty-four hours. Maybe I would work myself to death. A dear friend, who is also a relative, insists that I am a workaholic, something I deny vehemently. I rationalize that a workaholic does not know when to stop and I do. I have even been able to ignore chores, read a book, watch a movie, or just relax when I am not in the mood to do any chores. Are those the practices of a workaholic? I think not. On the contrary, I practice my Aunt Gertie's principle, "I met work when I was born, and I will die and leave it."

I believe I have been programmed during the era I was born. I cannot speak for all baby boomers, but I can speak for the pre-baby boomers and the baby boomers that were born in my family. We were inducted into the labor force from birth. My initial memories are those of work and work-related activities. I know I did not attend any daycare or pre-kindergarten programs because they did not exist in Cedar Grove where I was born and raised. I do know that my youngest brother, Franklyn, five years my junior, did attend the crèche at the clinic, a pre-school daycare program on the grounds of the St. James Anglican Church and School. In the right hand section of the property, immediately between the St. James Anglican Church and the St. James Anglican School, opposite the church's graveyard, Aunt Ada Phillips—Loretta, Popee, and Gilkes' aunt—supervised the children. I don't know what the inside looked like. I don't believe the children had little mats or blankets for nap time, nor do I remember seeing painted walls or mobiles hanging from the roof, or any of the superabundance of toys that overwhelm today's day care centers. I

The Early Years in Cedar Grove

don't even know what the children did there. I remember that Franklyn went there, and that he and Aunt Ada developed a special relationship so that after he had grown and she had retired, he would walk down her street—streets in Cedar Grove were not named—stop at her gate, and call out a greeting; then they would exchange pleasantries right there at the fence. I don't know if he even remembers what she taught them in the crèche. I think they were fed there, but I don't know what the food was.

What I do remember is that while Franklyn was at the crèche, I was in school. I don't know where George was. Maybe he was also at Aunt Ada's crèche. George is three years my junior. I remember being a little barefooted girl of four in a romper. I know I wasn't wearing pampers, because they had not arrived in Antigua yet. I knew as a baby that I wore diapers my mother had made. When they were soiled, she would wash, boil, and lay them out on the stone heap in the yard to bleach in the sun. She would then rinse them in water colored by a small square of blue that she had bought at the store. When dissolved in the water, the blue helps to whiten the whites; she would then hang spotless white diapers on the line. She taught this routine to my older sisters, who may have washed my diapers, but I never washed anyone's diapers. I was then promoted to cloth panties with elastic in the waist and legs, which my mother may have made. Who would have cared then? We had no overt or publicized incidents of child abuse. We had never heard of such things. If children wandered away from home, they were brought back unabused. Child abductions and the abuse of children were unheard of in our little corner of the world.

One day when my older siblings were running down the church hill to school, so that they could get in line before the school bell rang, I followed them. We lived at Barnes House, where I was born. From my memory, it was a huge shell with four wooden walls; the house was partitioned into living quarters minus the kitchen and bathroom. I know the kitchen was a separate building in the backyard, right in front of the most commonly used door. There was no step. In the place of steps, we would step on a huge rock, then up into the door. The latrine, our outdoor toilet, was a wooden building constructed over a deep hole, with a commode constructed over the hole. That was on the left corner of the property, closest to Mrs. Rachel

Henry's house. The kitchen was closest to Mary-Ann Sterling's house. We left Barnes House when Uncle Willie was murdered by his nephew, Dennis Heywood, popularly known as Windy. Windy was later hanged.

Barnes House was at the top of the hill, known as "Tapahill." The house was owned by Mr. Ervin Barnes, the wealthiest man in the village, from whom we were renting. From the front step, we looked straight down the road to the Cedar Grove and Hodges Bay Main Road. To the left was south Cedar Grove, known as Stevens with "Lapassa" on the eastern side. Behind us, over the hill, was Crosbies Estate where the Westcotts reigned supreme. On the immediate right was Teacher House, which may have been thus named because the headmaster of the school lived there. My siblings passed Teacher House, ran down the hill, keeping to the eastern side of the St. James Anglican Church, away from the graveyard, around the huge, brown iron water tank where we ran and hid while we played during recess. They were soon absorbed in the crowd of other children converging on the school grounds from all directions. No one seemed to notice me. I was the barefooted child in the romper, with or without underwear. I don't know how I escaped the headmaster's eyes, or the teachers' supervision, but I know that on a day in 1953 I entered the Cedar Grove School at the tender age of four, and I have been in school ever since.

Teacher Miriam, the teacher of the infant class, which would be equivalent to the pre-kindergarten class in the American educational system, may have kept me in her class because she knew I was another of the Knowles brood, or because she was my parents' friend. She was the godmother of my second brother, Ferdie. There were other barefooted students in the class, because our parents reserved our best pair of shoes for church and the other pair for school functions such as Empire Day and the Queen's Birthday celebration. I don't think those other children had entered school the same way I did. Their parents must have registered them, unlike mine. I got my slate, on which I learned penmanship. I listened to the stories Teacher Miriam read to us, and I learned about Mr. Willie, the pig. I learned the alphabet through the catchy tune with the letters, "ABCDEFG/ HIJKLMNOP/ QRSTU and V/ WXY and Z/ Now I've said my ABCs/ Won't you come and sing with me?" I learned the days of the week, the months of the year, and the times table to another tune, "Twice one is two/ Twice two is four/ Twice three is six/ And twice four is eight…." By the end of elementary school we had learned up to the twelve times table and I had learned to sound words. I learned to read, and I fell in love with reading.

    I stayed in school, learning and having fun, and I don't recall ever being registered. I now wonder if I just followed my siblings, or if I did actually get dressed and show up as a fully registered student. I don't recall my mother putting out my clothes as she would have done for the others, or if my older siblings were assigned that task. Those memories are buried in the far recesses somewhere, but I know I did go to school. That early entrance could have seriously affected my education and may have been the reason why I dropped out at the tender age of ten. But that is another story.

Chapter 2

Those Busy Fun-Filled Days

I continued school, which seemed to have been the highest point in my life. We had no TVs in the village. I don't know if there was any TV in Antigua. I don't even recall having heard the word before the 1960s, but that lapse could again be attributed to faulty memory. Some of us had radios, and we knew who those people were during cricket seasons because hordes of men would gather on the steps, at the windows, and even in the doorways of those houses that had radios. The radios were our entertainment outlets, our windows to the world, you may say.

Apart from the radios, we would have picture shows or film shows that many villagers referred to as "flim show." Periodically, some organization would bring the reels and we would have movie nights. Those were shown mainly in the schoolyard. The side of the building would be the screen on which someone would staple a large white sheet and we would sit on the ground, while the adults would bring chairs and benches to sit on. Most of our entertainment featured such characters as Sam the Cyclist, whose antics and slapstick comedy thrilled us and made us want to see him again and again.

There was the Deluxe Theater on High Street in St. John's, where it still is, but I have never been there. There was no religious prohibition for us; I think my mother's moral code superseded all other mandates because it had never entered my mind to request to go to the movies, and I don't think any of my sisters did either. I know that my brother Ferdie frequented the Deluxe Theater because he talked about it in his manner, as only a dumb person could, without the assistance of the British or American Sign Language. His antics, which were always punctuated by sounds of shooting, told me that he had seen a lot of western movies. John Wayne had become his favorite movie star. Now that I think about it, the theater wasn't the place for young ladies to go, and we were examples, paragons of virtue for the young ladies in the village; Ros, P, Mave, Hazel, and Valerie were the cream of the crop. So we listened to the radio; we entertained ourselves and flocked to the St. James School grounds when the pictures were brought to us.

However, we never felt deprived. We were very happy, busy doing our chores, which included learning to do all the domestic things like keeping the house clean, doing the laundry, learning to cook and bake, keeping the yard clean, and even growing flowers at home because we were growing food for our home use as well as for commercial purposes at the "ground," which was land we cultivated out of the village. Every morning during the week we would wend our way to various estates: Royal, Tarn Gilla (Tom Gilead), or Seventeen, where we worked lands that we did not own. I didn't quite understand how it was done because, "Children were to be seen and not heard," and we were not to be too inquisitive to question our parents about adult business. The closest relationship I can ally that with is sharecropping. My mother leased the land from someone, primarily the government, and we worked it, planting our food crops, sugarcane, cotton, or whatever was producing money at the time. And as if those locations were not enough, we would also go to Powell's Estate, to plant cotton and then harvest it on my father's property. But those sites were not all. My mother decided that we needed more work to keep us busy, so she took a job farming for the Shouls. I remember weeding the rows at Santy, above Royal Pond. They were the longest rows I've ever hoed.

Anyway, every weekday morning, before we went to school at 9:00 a.m., we would put in a few hours at one of our grounds weeding, planting, or thinning out plants. I'm amazed that so many of my students experience difficulty getting to class on time for nine o'clock, when we had to do so much work and still get to school on time before the bell rang. I wonder if the days were longer then than they are now. Then, after school we would head back to the field until sunset. It was not as laborious as it sounds, but it was a lot of work. We had fun at times.

Every summer, our vacation was spent in the fields where we would reap the corn and roast some of it right there. Someone would conveniently have a bag with some brown sugar, and we would have roasted corn covered in brown sugar. What a treat! When we finished harvesting our corn, we would go to Uncle Eddy and Daphne's field and harvest theirs as well, while their children stayed at home because they were too refined to work in the field, even in their own. We dried some of the corn, then shelled the grains off the stalk, parched them in the yabba—a large clay baking dish—then ground them in the mortar and pestle and made a snack called ashum—dried and roasted ground corn mixed with a little nutmeg and sugar. What a treat that was! I was enlightened when, as a student at the Antigua Girls High School, I learned from the town girls that they made ashum by toasting yellow cornmeal, then adding sugar. I always wondered what it tasted like, but I never really tried it. Why would I when we always had corn? Roasting the corn was a routine activity that provided a meal or a snack for us. There were times when we were harvesting sweet potatoes, and we would take smoke herring to the field, and there we would roast sweet potatoes and smoke herring. My mouth still waters years later as I think of that treat. We worked hard, but we had fun.

Sometimes we would be having so much fun that the time literally got away from us before we could complete the assigned tasks. One such day was a cotton planting day. My mother, like all the other farmers, planted by the *McDonald's Almanac,* which indicated the positions of the moon and the most favorable times for planting to yield bountiful harvests. In addition to the almanac, our parents insisted that we should always plant seeds on full bellies, especially when we were planting corn so that the ears would be big and full. You would think following the almanac would have been enough to produce big, full ears, but I think they wanted a full guarantee. We were planting cotton seed, and we had to have full bellies, so we decided to cook and eat at Royal's because we did not have time to eat at home after school. After we got home from school, our routine was to change from our school clothes into field clothes, get some water, the bag of cotton seeds, our hoes, and head out. At Royal's, we started the fire, dug the potatoes—getting the small spuds, because we could eat those in their skin, and we didn't want to eat the profit—and we roasted the smoke herring. We insisted on eating before planting, so while we waited for dinner we scrounged around for ripe watermelons and feasted on them. Then it was dinner time. There is only so much time between 3:00 p.m. and sunset. Before we knew it the sun was setting and we hadn't planted the field of cotton. There was no way we could have planted the whole field and gotten home before dark, so we decided to cheat. We were instructed to plant three seeds in each hole, so we wouldn't have much thinning to do later. We pretended to have forgotten that bit of advice because to finish quickly we started pouring fistfuls of seeds into holes. By sunset we had emptied a bag of cotton seeds.

All went well; we forgot about our prodigal behavior until a few weeks later when the seeds began to germinate. I don't recall the precise punishment, but knowing my mother, I am sure we got licks, all of us. We also had to thin the cotton seedlings and plant them in the section of the field that we had ignored. I don't recall, but I know we had a bumper harvest that year, so we must have compensated for our misdeeds.

Chapter 3

Long Live the Apprenticeship System!

I was born on the cusp of a great period in the Caribbean when the apprenticeship system was still in vogue. I was the eighth of eleven children, with five sisters and five brothers. My sisters Ros and P went to learn embroidery and sewing from Teacher Sybil. Mave was at Uncle Eddy's and his wife, Daphne, cleaning the duck pond and helping out in the house. Later, she and I went to Mrs. Francis to learn typing and shorthand. Mave also took music lessons with Teacher Mary, our cousin. Hazel helped out at her Godmother Ernie's, who was married to our cousin Denzil George. Ferdie and Everette worked with Papa. By the time I started running around Cedar Grove, Wilmouth, our oldest sibling, had left home for Barbuda, where he grew up with our maternal grandfather.

This "helping out" was an informal application of the apprenticeship system, where we learned practical skills as we assisted the professionals. I don't remember being farmed out to anyone, but I can recall very clearly being Mr. Roseau's errand girl. Mr. Roseau, the father of Wilmouth, my oldest brother, later became my father's best friend and our neighbor. He operated the corner shop and lived across the street in a huge house. That property was adjacent to our house, separated only by an old fence. My father spent most of his nonworking days there in the yard, which was one huge garage, with Mr. Roseau tinkering, stripping old cars to get parts for the vehicles they were working on. Mrs. Peters, whom we called Freda Peters, cooked Mr. Roseau's dinner, and it was my responsibility to collect it and take it to him. I also ran other errands for him.

Mrs. Peters ran a shop on the southern end of the village, which accommodated the villagers from Eight House, Longfords, and those areas,

Long Live the Apprenticeship System!

but our parents shopped where the prices were best. We lived close to Doctor Peters and his family who ran a shop, but because we were friends and nearly related to the Barnes family we had an account at Teacher Fanny's shop. That did not prevent us from shopping at the other shops. There seemed to be an unwritten and unspoken rule about doing business at the village shops. We had an account at Teacher Fanny's shop, so we would take goods on credit, but every Saturday night we would pay off that bill and begin a new account. On some Saturday nights when we were sent to the shop to get our groceries, I would hear children say that their mothers weren't ready to pay the past week's bill, but they would like to buy the groceries for the coming week, "But Mama will pay next week because her hand is short." I could never understand how that worked, but they got their groceries. However, if we ran short of something, or if we wanted a quick purchase, we would run over to Doctor Peters' shop. When groceries were scarce, we would shop around at all the shops where the shopkeepers rationed their goods. Sometimes they "married" them, so that if flour was scare, but there were lots of potatoes, they would say that we could get flour only if we bought potatoes.

Those were the days when the village literally raised us. We were our parents' children by conception and by birth, but the village had full authority to discipline us, to order us about as their messengers, and to report our misdeeds to our parents. The village also fed us and nurtured us. Our mother taught us when we went to play at our friends' homes that we should always leave at dinner time, so that they would not be obligated to feed us because we were all in the same financial situations. We adhered to those rules; if, perchance, we were at a neighbor's home when a meal was being served, we would be invited to share, even if it meant that someone—and it was usually a parent—would go without a meal. If a parent happened to leave home without indicating the day's rations, we children didn't have to worry; we knew we would have been fed not only by our relatives, but by the neighbors in the village.

I was Mr. Roseau's unpaid servant. I ran his errands; I collected his meals, and I returned the empty dishes to Mrs. Peters. I don't recall ever sweeping his house or washing dishes. I ran errands. One day when I was about nine-years-old, I was playing with my cousins Janet and Anita, who lived in our "yard" on the same piece of property. We were the grandchildren of Alice Mascall, whose family owned the property from one street to another. We lived on the Cedar Grove main road in the house that had belonged to her brother, Willie Mascall. Uncle Willie never married and had no children, so my mother, Winifred, took care of him. She prepared his meals, did his laundry, and helped him keep his house clean. When he was killed by his nephew Dennis, my mother inherited his property, so we left Barnes House and moved into our own house, though it was much smaller.

To the left of our house was my grandmother's sister's house, Aunt Edith's house. She was Dennis's mother. Several feet from that house was Uncle Victor's house, my grandmother's brother, but he never lived there. He chose to live in the village with his family while my Aunt Appin occupied his house. Across the yard from his house was my grandmother's house. We called her Aunt Alice, even though she was our grandmother. On the other end of the property, bordering the other street was Maggie's house; my grandmother's other sister, whom we called Dadda. To the right of her house was her only son's house. Denzil and his wife, Ernie, had been childless for a very long time, so we children in the yard were treated as their children until Patty and Italas were born. The whole yard was one big family, and we wandered freely in and out of the houses. Sometimes we even slept where night found us. No one needed to worry about us because they knew we would have been well cared for, with all our physical and even emotional needs met. One shout from any house would have assured a parent or sibling of our whereabouts.

One day I was playing with my cousins and with Cicely from across the street. Her mother was my mother's best friend. I don't recall what we were playing, but I knew it was a game that required us to run all around the houses, into the alley, and back to base without being caught. We were swift then. While we were playing, I heard, "Valerie, Valerie!" At that moment, I didn't want to hear Mr. Roseau's voice at all. I didn't want to leave my friends. I didn't want to leave my game. But an adult had called, and I had to respond immediately.

So I replied, left my friends and the game, and rushed into Mr. Roseau's yard. In my haste, I confronted him and shouted, "Mr. Roseau, see me ya."

Without acknowledging my presence, he demanded, "How dare you speak to me like that?"

I was shocked into realization. I had forgotten to switch from my dialect, which I was speaking with my friends, to the standard language, the only language we were allowed to speak to adults and authority figures. I had to apologize profusely before Mr. Roseau felt he could entrust his mission to my dialect-speaking mouth. He wanted to know that the lips that requested his Phensic or Whiz tablets from the little village store would honor him and my parents. I have never forgotten that afternoon. There were many other members of my village of Cedar Grove whose diligent attention and high expectations helped me maintain high values and set high standards for myself.

The village was the backdrop to our activities. We were country people even though we were only four and a half miles north of the capital city, St. John's. Some even thought of us as country bumpkins and showed great surprise when they actually met us and realized that we looked like them, dressed like them, and even talked like them. Well, not really. We did not have that city-talking twang. During my first year at the Antigua Girls High School, an older student, Barbara, overheard a conversation I had with some friends, who were also country girls from the southeastern villages of Liberta and English Harbour. She said, "You don't talk like a country girl." I wondered what she had expected a country girl to sound like, but I didn't care enough to ask.

One of the mentors and role models in our village was Mrs. Frances Barnes, affectionately called Teacher Fanny because she had taught for many years before she married the furniture maker, business tycoon, and first funeral undertaker in Antigua, Mr. Ervin Barnes. When I became her protégée, Teacher Fanny was the mother of four grown children and the owner of the best shop in Cedar Grove. She taught me how to behave like a young lady and how to deport myself accordingly. She was the teacher of my Sunday School class at the Anglican Church. To this day, I remember the songs and scriptures she taught us to memorize as well as the lessons in humility and love that she not only taught, but lived by. On one occasion when she was called a country person, she retorted in her characteristic manner, "I may be from the country, but I am not countrified." That stopped the person in their tracks. Very early in my life, I learned that I was of great value and that there was a whole village of people who were looking out for me. Because our parents couldn't be everywhere, God provided the village to undertake the responsibilities of our parents, a role they fulfilled very well.

Because the villagers were our guardians, we owed them the same respect and attention that we owed our parents. At no time could we fail to acknowledge adults or express the appropriate greetings. Nor could we display unmannerly behaviors in their presence. Because "girls were to be seen and not heard," we deported ourselves well, showing the greatest respect and honor to the neighbors. Should we fail to honor that unwritten law, we would suffer the consequences. It amazed us all as children how, in a community where there were only two telephones, how quickly news spread around the village. If some of us failed to show the expected respect to an adult on our way home, and we walked or ran straight home, when we arrived our mother—and it was always the mother—would meet us at the door with the strap or a tamarind switch. How did she learn of the disrespect? How did that bit of news get to her ahead of us when we had gone straight home? It still baffles some of us.

My mother would beat, discipline, and then listen to the explanation or the real version. We dared not suggest that an adult had lied, so we would circumvent the expression by claiming misunderstanding on someone's part. I must admit that for the greater part the adults were good to us, except my mother's best friend. She lived just across the street with her four children, her mother, whom we called Aunt Joyce, and for a while her mother's brother, whom we called Uncle Bobby. Her two older girls, Lynn and Avril, were our cousins, the daughters of my mother's brother Uncle Eddy. My mother's friend announced to the village that she didn't set any watchmen over her children, so she refused to listen to any complaints made on her children. My mother, however, failed to follow her friend's role, and she punished us whenever her friend complained, which was often and usually distorted.

After her friend's accusation we would be punished, but after my

Long Live the Apprenticeship System!

mother had cooled down, we could talk to her, giving her our version, which was the correct version. We called our mother Darling. I don't know who started calling her that, but by the time I was born it was well established, so I fell in line. Darling guarded her reputation zealously, and her children were an extension of her honor, so we had to deport ourselves to meet those standards. That was a primary reason for her getting into a rage when her friend reported on us. We had disappointed her. After the heat of the moment, we would explain to her what had happened, and instead of apologizing, she would use one of her many proverbs, "Where there's smoke there's fire." That continued until the day when she encountered one of her nieces, her friend's oldest daughter, in a compromising situation. As the aunt and best friend of the mother, she thought it was her duty to report the incident. To her chagrin, her friend shut her up by reminding her, "I don't set any watchman over my children." That was enough to teach my mother her lesson. From that day onward, whenever Baby Joe made any complaints on us, Darling would listen respectfully, thank her for being a good neighbor, and dismiss it. She thought it was very strange that someone who didn't want to have anyone report on her children would always be reporting on other people's children. This did not seem to affect their relationship, for they continued to be friends.

Chapter 4

Of Manners and Behaviors

My mother was a wonder, but I did not realize it until much later. I don't think any of us children realized what an unusual mother she was. She was strict. She demanded respect of her children, and she expected us to display that same behavior to others, even her enemies. In Cedar Grove Village where we lived, we knew that we were to respect all adults, whether they were our parents' friends or not. There was one family that seemed to be at enmity with my family. Mrs. B seemed to be the common enemy. She was not on speaking terms with our grandmother or with our mother and her sisters. As a matter of fact, she was not on speaking terms with anyone in our yard. With any of the adults, that is. Our parents' enemies were not our enemies. That was very clearly conveyed to us. Adults and children were not on the same level; consequently, children had no business in adults' affairs. That was clearly expressed in the saying that we heard so very often, "That's why children and adults are not buried in the same place." We were led to believe that the graveyard was segregated, separating adults from children.

Even though we knew that Mrs. B was not our mother's friend, we dared not lose our common sense and disrespect her. When we met her, we had to respectfully greet her by saying, "Good morning, Mrs. B," and continue on our way. If she requested our help, we were duty bound to offer our assistance very cheerfully. Should we fail to obey her, she, our mother's enemy, would walk up to our home, call our mother, and lay our misdeeds at her feet. And our mother, our darling mother, would discipline us in her presence to show that she did not condone our behavior. What an age in which we were raised! Mrs. B would then proceed on her way, and she would still be my mother's enemy. I am pleased to say that I lived to see that feud between our family and Mrs. B resolved.

Of Manners and Behaviors

After Teacher Fanny retired from her shop, she leased it to my mother, who ventured into business. It was quite a change from farming the fields, but we did not really give up the fields. I liked the shop. I liked weighing and bagging the dry goods. I liked waiting on the customers who came daily to purchase their goods, most often on credit. After I had completed my General Certificate of Examination (GCE) "O" Level, while I waited for college acceptance, I ran the shop. Since the shop was on the northern part of the village in Lapassa, I walked from our home through the village, stopping to greet all I met along the way, and stopping to visit with my relatives in the yard. By the time I got to the shop many customers knew I had gone to open up and they were there waiting for me. I hated that. I liked to arrive at the shop about 7:30 a.m., which looked very late during the summer months. I would open one door, open the windows, sweep the shop and the steps, dust off the counter and the shelved goods, get out the book and date it, and then I would open the other door. Only after all this would the shop be officially open for business.

As I awaited my customers, I would check each section to ensure enough bagged goods were ready to be distributed. I also made sure that the cans and bottles of goods were clean and well displayed to attract our customers. When Teacher Fanny ran the shop, I used to wish I had access to the many toffees, chewing gums, and chocolate candies. When I ran the shop, I realized that I soon got tired of the things I used to crave. I would sit and read. Oh how I read that summer. I had a sparse but valuable collection. Every year at The Antigua Girls High School we had Speech Day, which was the day when the students with the highest grade point averages (GPA) were recognized and awarded. Since I was the student with the highest GPA in each form I progressed to, I received books every year. During my third form year my Latin teacher, Mrs. Winifred F. V. Cooke, presented me with a huge book of the best American short stories. I read that book from cover to cover. I think it was that book that ignited the flame for John Steinbeck, Ernest Hemingway, Willa Cather, Flannery O'Connor, Edgar Allan Poe, and T. S. Eliot. I ran the shop and I read. I read as I ran the shop. That was a summer that I will never forget.

The shop was in Mrs. B's neighborhood and before I knew it, she was a customer. Before long when my mother would pay her periodic visit, she and Mrs. B would sit on the step and talk as if they had been lifelong friends. We children commented on it, and when we got Darling in a good mood, we would wonder aloud about what could have brought about the end of the feud. I don't think anyone ever apologized or attempted to resolve the conflict.

One day to my surprise, which I had to conceal, Mrs. B appeared at the step and instead of climbing up she sat down, complaining about her "bad knees," and asked if we had smoke herring. Despite my great surprise I wished her a good afternoon and informed her that we indeed had smoke herring that we had received the previous evening. I wondered if she really wanted smoke herring or if she was trying to worm her way into our business. She bought a few skinless smoke herrings, muttering under her breath, "I hope I have enough. As soon as you put these things in hot water they seem to shrink away." I wanted to ask if she was thinking of buying enough for her whole family, because I thought with Mr. Belle and seven growing children she had better buy more smoke herring. Of course I didn't know if she fed her children the way our mother fed us. I thought maybe that was why the children were so scrawny.

When Darling learned that Mrs. B had actually come to the shop to buy something she smiled, but said nothing. Before long, she and Mrs. B were hanging out on the shop step, and before we realized it, the whole Lake family—Mrs. B's sisters, and brother—and my mother and all the ladies in the yard were friends. That friendship continued. Mrs. B would often stop at our home to talk or to complain about her husband, Mr. B. I liked Mr. B. He was so very different from his wife in the fact that while she accumulated enemies, he collected friends. Mr. B was everybody's friend. He was a very handsome man and even though he was old, my parents' age, he looked very well and dressed very sharply. It was alleged that he was a ladies' man, but we children would sympathize with him and condone his behavior because we thought he had a virago for a wife. Later, when Mrs. B became our mother's friend, we started thinking more favorably of her. We actually liked her. She was the aunt of our cousins Melrose and Gillian, her sister's children, who were the children of my mother's brother, Uncle Eddy. The close family ties that existed in the village never ceased to amaze us. Almost all of us were related and those who were not related to us were related to our relatives.

Of Manners and Behaviors

The summer I ran the shop was my excellent introduction into the world of business. It taught me the importance of service, and I learned that service is not servitude. When I would be in the shop Teacher Fanny would stop by. I wondered how she always seemed to visit when the shop was empty and I was alone. I thought those times may have been her free periods when she ran the shop. Those were the times when she would drop her pearls of wisdom in her very quiet, yet matronly way. She started by praising me for the good work I had been doing. She said everyone who visited her talked of how businesslike and respectful I was. Then she warned me about the families who never seemed to have money to pay their bills and she told me to always let the customers pay off their existing bills before I created new accounts for them. She would end in her typical manner, with her lips puckered up, "Remember that your mother has to pay Mr. Aska when he brings the goods. If she does not collect from her creditors, how will she be able to pay her debts?" With that, she would grab her cane and slowly saunter back to her home at the northeast corner of the shop.

There was an unwritten law that all adult relatives should be called Uncle or Aunt. To this day we have so many uncles, such as Uncle Percy, and aunts such as Aunt Lav and Aunt Myrtle, who were not biological aunts and uncles. They were older relatives, so we had to extend the courtesy and refer to them as aunt and uncle.

My mother was the first of seven children. Her father was Elisha Francis, better known as Monty Francis, who was a Barbudan, so she spent most of her youth in Barbuda. Her siblings were Uncle Eddy, Uncle Ivan, Uncle Irving, Fernie, and Appin—whom we've never called Aunt. The fourth brother died as a child, but even though we did not know him we learned a lot about Selvin. They were the children of Lennie Barnes, brother of Ervin Barnes, which gave us the close relationship with the Barnes family. My mother was a tall woman who must have grown bigger with each birth she gave because I have always known her as a well-built woman, even though pictures of her in her youth showed a thin, tall lady. Both my parents were about the same height and build and often people would regard them as brother and sister.

Darling was a quiet speaker who usually thought through her words before expressing them. She was a thinker and a planner. She taught us to always plan for a "rainy day" because it was better to say, "Here it is" than to ask, "Where is it?" In her use of proverbs she taught us to listen well, think through our actions, and talk very little. She taught us that, "A still tongue keepeth a wise head." She taught us the principles of relationship by uttering one proverb, "Run not too frequently into your neighbors' house because they will grow to hate you." She instilled excellent domestic skills by reminding us that, "Cleanliness is next to Godliness." Every day before we left home she reminded us to make the beds and clean the house because, "you don't know if you will get sick and people will have to bring you home." Another reminder in that vein was as follows, "Always wear clean and good underwear because you don't know what may happen to you while you are out."

She taught us the meaning of sacrifice by sacrificing much for us. She denied herself many things so that her children would have their needs met. She taught us the difference between needs and wants. She would say the following, "Wants are things that you can live without. When you need something, you have to have it. That is important." We learned to be satisfied with our possessions and not to envy others.

She taught us to invest in quality. When I attended the Antigua Girls High School, every summer my mother took me to show me how to buy my school shoes and other supplies. She always made the uniforms. During those times she would select sturdy leather shoes that lasted several years. One year she gave me $30 and entrusted the task of buying school shoes to me. I went from store to store, checking prices and trying on shoes. The prices ranged from $15 to $29.99 and I reasoned that they looked the same. I bought a lovely pair of shoes for $15 and was proud that I had saved so much money. When I displayed my purchase Darling looked at them and told me, very patiently, that they were not leather and she questioned their durability. She allowed me to wear my shoes and just as she had predicted, they fell apart before the end of the second quarter of the school year. She said not a word, but suggested that I resort to the shoes from the former year. To this day I examine the quality of purchases before investing.

Of Manners and Behaviors

Darling was a typical mother of her time; she did not talk to us about the birds and the bees, but her proverbs were reminders that, "good things come to those who wait." The most outstanding trait that I admired in my mother was her openness and her ability to listen to us. We knew when she was vexed we had to be very careful and stay out of her way. After she got over her anger we would talk to her and explain the situation. I seldom see that quality in adults and I was always happy that Darling had a rapport with us and allowed us to explain ourselves. This is a quality that we should extend to our children.

Chapter 5

Religion Permeated Our Lives

Growing up in Cedar Grove was exciting. In addition to the work we always had to do, we led very active religious lives. One of the headmasters at the St. James School was Mr. Lawrence Richards, who was also a lay reader in the Anglican Church. I don't know if there was any connection between his being an Anglican lay reader and also the headmaster of an Anglican school, but he sure made good use of that church. Those were the days when church buildings were opened daily so that people could go in to pray or meditate in a quiet place. Some visitors, who could have been tourists, also liked to visit churches, and I could understand why. The church had been built during slavery, with very thick walls. It was constructed in the shape of a cross. Every week the members of the Mother's Union would clean the church and polish the benches, lecterns, and the silver communion set. It was an old church, a simple church, but it was well maintained. Even the graveyard was kept clean.

Norman and Egen were the sextons and the minister's assistant. Norman was an old man when I knew him. He worked for Freda Peters during the week, running her errands and minding her sheep. Every morning he would limpingly walk the herd of sheep to Crawford's where they would graze, sometimes getting as far as Royal's Estate. In the afternoon he would reverse his steps as he brought the sheep home. Norman rang the church bell to alert us of the times for worship. Seated at the back of the church, across the aisle from the baptismal font, was the last bench where Mrs. Warner would sit with Norman. One Sunday, Mr. Hewlett, a lay reader, preached at the Anglican Church, and some of us were complaining about how boring he was. As we passed Mrs. Warner she addressed us and told us that we must respect all speakers and try to get the message from their sermons. She concluded by saying, "Even if old man Norman were to preach, I'd listen and get a blessing." Norman's preaching was something to be considered, but we soon dismissed her good counsel.

Mr. Richards introduced an annual play in the school and an annual cantata. To practice for the cantata we would walk to the church in single file. When we got there we would sit in our classes and either Teacher Geraldine or Teacher Miriam would play the organ while we sang. Mr. Richards was a solfege musician, so he would have us first practice doh-re-mi-fa-so-lah, then doh-doh-doh-lah-ti-fa, until he felt we were ready to put the parts together. The whole village would attend those cantatas, dressed in their Sunday best, and we sang as harmoniously as angels.

The plays were something else. The St. James Anglican School, also known as the Cedar Grove School, was a huge structure, built in the shape of the cross, like the church. The top of the cross had a raised platform that was used as a stage. This was where Mr. Richards' desk was. That was his open office. On the right side of the cross were Standards III, IV, and V. On the left were Standards I and II. The bottom of the cross housed the infant class. There were no partitions. It was one huge open space with approximately 150 students and four teachers. The principal engaged in classes from 9:00 a.m. to 3:00 p.m. with recess in the morning and afternoon, and lunch break in the middle. That must have been pandemonium, but we learned quite a lot. There was no privacy, so discipline, which was usually administered by the strap, was always a spectator sport. So were the rehearsals for the play. Who would pay attention to teachers when other students were rehearsing for the play? That was our time to observe and comment, sometimes very loudly.

I was a little girl in one play. I was Victoria and Gertrude Francis was my mother. I don't recall who the other characters were; I don't even recall the title of the play, but I do recall that I had to tell my mother that Grandpa, who had been considered dead, was waking up. It must have gone well because all of Mr. Richards' plays were great hits with the villagers, but that's the extent of my memory.

We were busy before we got to school in the mornings; we were busy at school, and we were busy after school farming. You would think we would be eagerly anticipating the weekends, which we were, for various reasons.

We didn't go to the grounds during the weekends. My mother went to town on Saturday mornings to sell produce from the grounds or to drop off orders. When those were done she would shop for the week. While she was gone we had to clean the whole house, which included cleaning the glass windows with newspaper and vinegar until they shone and polishing our mahogany furniture with O Cedar polish. When I was too young to clean the house, I would wend my way to the end of the road above Mr. Roseau's shop where Sister Satterfield conducted Advent Sabbath School. It seemed to have been an offshoot of the Seventh-day Adventist Church, but we liked going there, not only to learn about Jesus' love for us, but also because every Saturday Mr. Jardine would ride into the village from St. John's with bags of baked goods on the passenger seat of his motorcycle. Among those goodies were the pastries filled with red coconut that we called bun tarts. At the end of each Advent Sabbath class each child received a huge bun tart that we would eat on our way home.

Our Dadda Maggie was a Seventh-day Adventist, so every Sabbath; she would dress in her Sabbath best, push in her door, put a stone behind it, and saunter off to church. Some of us in the yard would accompany her, but when we were reminded of the bun tarts that Sister Sat, as we affectionately called her, distributed, we chose to attend Advent Sabbath in the morning and after lunch, accompany Dadda to M.V. at her church. M.V. was the abbreviation for Missionary Volunteer meeting, which catered to the young people and children. We didn't get bun tarts at the Adventist Church, but we liked the socials that they would sponsor on Saturday nights on the church grounds where we would play games, my favorite being "Steal Miss Liza." We would form a ring; then a boy or young man would start singing the song, "I'm one boy without a girl," and we would respond with, "Steal Liza Jane." He would continue, "I have no one to call my own," and we would admonish him to, "Steal Liza Jane." As he sang he would walk around the ring eyeing the girls, then he would stand in front of the one he fancied and she would be his girl for the duration of the game. We called the game Adventist dance because some of the boys and girls were very active as they danced around the ring making their selections. Their creative walks seemed to defy the artistic prancing and jumping of professional choreographers. Whenever I think of "Steal Miss Liza," I think of Bobby Kirby, a chubby gentleman who would exercise every part of his body as he pranced, bobbed, and weaved on his way to his girl and also while he escorted her back to his space in the ring.

On Sunday morning, we would don our Sunday best, our one pair of church shoes, and head down the hill to the Anglican Church where we were christened, and where we walked for confirmation, and were eventually confirmed. As we grew older we became members of the choir and were very active in the church. When the Anglican service ended we would stop on the way at the Christian Mission Church, which was officially named the Pilgrim Holiness Church. There we would be taught a memory verse that we had to recite to our parents before we could be given our Sunday dinner. On that same day we would also attend the Moravian Church because Aunt Ada had given us poems to be recited at their annual Missionary Program, so we had to rehearse. Sometimes the Moravian Church would have religious movies such as Nebuchadnezzar's *Golden Image*. That also was an event that brought out nearly the whole village.

Our Sunday dinner was always special. We did not seem to mind that on Sundays we had only two meals because Sunday breakfast was a culinary undertaking. We would have stewed salt fish with hard boiled eggs, chopped up cooked eggplants, spinach, okras, fried buggaments, the short fat plantain that grew in Antigua, the biggest ti ti bread—so called because of the two pointed ends that resemble a female's breasts—that Mrs. Davis made with the braided plaits, and as many cups of chocolate tea as we craved. My mother sold chocolate sticks, so she would buy the cocoa beans and roast them in the yabba. After they cooled we would shell them. She would then grind the roasted cocoa beans in the mortar and pestle. After a few years she graduated to the stones. She would have a smooth, large, flat stone on the table, place the roasted, shelled beans on the stone, and then crush them with a smaller stone. That process was very messy, since the oil from the ground beans would splatter all over the kitchen. Finally, she bought a manually operated meat grinder that she used to grind the cocoa. It was a greasy affair. I recall that some of the customers would accuse her of putting sweet oil in the chocolate, which we defended royally.

At home we would cook the broken chocolates or the ones that resisted her manipulations. Sometimes the ground cocoa would get too soft and Darling had to let it harden. We didn't have a refrigerator; that would have solved the problem by hardening the cocoa, but I guess it taught us patience. After such a sumptuous breakfast, we had to walk off the effects. It's no wonder we went to all those churches!

Sunday dinner was another feat. My mother would cook the big iron pot full of rice and pigeon peas, grown on our rented land; that would be served with stewed beef, or goat, or a chicken we had killed; peas and carrots; boiled sweet potatoes sliced, and potato salad or baked macaroni and cheese. Years later while I was a student at the Antigua Girls High School I discovered that all thirty-six girls in my class had the same dinner each Sunday, with variations between beef and store-bought chicken. I don't recall dessert, nor do I recall the mandatory drink. However, our drink of choice was limeade made of water, sugar, and limes, which we affectionately called "brebitch," an adulteration of beverage. Fish was never served on Sundays. Saltfish and smoke herring were acceptable breakfast entrees, but they would never be served for Sunday dinner. Sometimes we would attend Sunday evening service at church, or if an evangelistic series was being held at the Pilgrim Holiness Church, we would go to listen to the hell fire preachers and join in the choruses, which we liked to sing.

If there was no action that required us to venture from our home, we would sit on the front steps, joined by some of our neighbors, and tell stories. Sometimes Gusta Lynch would bring out her ice cream freezer and make ice cream, which she sold at the corner near the Pilgrim Holiness Church. We would buy a cone of ice cream for six pence or as much as twenty-five cents. Sometimes we took our enamel cups for the ice cream because we thought we got more than if we had bought a cone. We would return home and tell riddles, with the prize for the winner being a bag of roast corn and sugar or ashum. Those were the days when we did not have electricity. Most of the homes were lit by kerosene lamps, whose shades we had to clean each morning. To create a cleaner, shinier lamp shade, we would put a little corn meal in the shade and swipe it around with the rag.

Religion Permeated Our Lives

Some homes were lit by flambeaux, which were soda bottles with kerosene oil with cloth wicks protruding from the mouths of the bottles. You can imagine how dirty those house roofs became as the flambeaux emitted those dark flames.

Chapter 6

Education, My First Love

When Mr. Richards was transferred to another school, Mr. Alister Francis became the new headmaster. I had been promoted to the third standard, so I may have been about nine years old. Every Monday morning the first assignment was penmanship for the whole school, which would be the copying of a proverb or a few lines of poetry that each teacher would have written on the class blackboard. We were encouraged to present our best penmanship. After the assigned time each teacher would look at the students' writing and would correct imperfect formations of letters with red ink. We would then parade class-by-class before Mr. Francis' desk. Any book that had a red mark earned the student a few blows from his strap.

Mr. Francis was a young strapping man whose blows hurt the back. I knew because I was his victim. I grew to hate Monday morning penmanship, and I hated the blows even more. I thought it was so unfair. Why should we be punished for doing our best? I couldn't take another blow from that strap, so I stopped attending school. I don't know what transpired between my parents and the school, but I do know that I was accompanying my mother to the grounds daily and that I was earning my keep by working hard. I would weed the bush and devil grass with my little hoe, and I was very handy in providing water to the thirsty adults. I even became the fastest cotton picker on my father's property at Powell's Estate. I don't recall how long my truancy continued, but by the new school year an energetic young man came to teach at the school. He was our cousin Joseph Hampson.

My paternal grandmother Jane Ann Elvin married my grandfather George Knowles and they lived at Powell's Estate. Her sister, Christiana Elvin, married George Hampson, and they lived at New Winthorpes, two villages away from Powell's. Granny died when I was four years old, but my memories of her revolve around the kitchen. She always seemed to be in the kitchen. I guess when she had to feed a husband and five men with voracious appetites she and her daughters, Aunt Gertie and Aunt Mollie, had to spend much time in the kitchen, so later, when those children had made their homes, the kitchen was a refuge for her. Granny died, but her sister Aunt Narna, as we affectionately called her, reminded me of my grandmother every time I visited her. Joseph, Aunt Narna's grandson, lived across the road from her, so any visit to Aunt Narna would mean seeing the family across the street.

Joseph boarded with his Aunt Hilda, Mrs. Joseph, who was married to the pilot from Cedar Grove, who was a member of the Pilgrim Holiness Church. Brother Clarence, as he was known, had one of the two telephones in the village. He was the ships' pilot and he had to be accessible to bring the vessels into the harbor. The other telephone was owned by the Barnes family. Mr. Barnes was the funeral undertaker and had to be accessible when death struck. When Joseph arrived in Cedar Grove our house was one of his first stops because we were family. It was then that he discovered I was not attending school and he informed my mother that I had to return to school. In those days the teachers' words were law. And it was not just any teacher; this was Mr. Joseph Hampson, our cousin. He started by giving me lessons to help me catch up with what I had missed. During that process, he claimed that I was a bright girl and he redoubled his efforts to prove that I was intelligent. *The Student's Companion* became my constant companion, and I developed the habit of memorizing historical facts. Joseph introduced me to the classics by lending me books from his library. I started reigniting my love of reading.

I re-entered school; there was no fanfare. I had dropped out, and then I returned. I started to excel and Joseph had greater plans for me. When my sisters Mave and Hazel completed Cedar Grove School, they transferred to an all-girls public school—Girls School—in St. John's, where they continued their education. By that time Wilmouth, Ferdie, Everette, Ros, and P had ended school and were working. Joseph continued working with me and after one year I too was transferred to Girls School. I was placed in Teacher Molly's class and she continued from where Joseph had left off. I wrote voluminous notes from the board and memorized the poems that

Teacher Molly taught us as we sat on the ground around the east Country Pond that landscaped the school ground. My favorite poem was "The Wreck of the Hesperus" by Henry Wadsworth Longfellow. I borrowed books from Teacher Molly, who was very generous, and I regained my love for learning. At the end of that year I took the common entrance examination given to all eleven-year-olds in Antigua. I scored the highest. The three highest scorers of the exam were given scholarships to the Antigua Girls High School. Thus began the happiest five years of my education.

The Antigua Girls High School was originally a parochial school run by the Anglican Church. It was the school where the British plantation owners and wealthy Antiguans sent their daughters to be educated. The ownership shifted from the Anglican Church to the Antiguan government in 1960. However, the student population remained the same and most of the teachers came from England, Scotland, and Wales. Erma Potter, Vanessa Matthew, and I were the scholarship recipients who began school in January of 1962. Today, Erma remains my best friend in Antigua. When we entered the grounds of the Antigua Girls High School we encountered our British headmistress, Miss Lorna Blake. She demanded the respect of all girls and she modeled perfect deportment to us. Our arithmetic and algebra teacher and our Bible Doctrines teacher were Miss Helen Goodwin and Miss Mamie Branch. They were both respectively daughters of Antiguan white population and were themselves old girls of the Antigua Girls High School. Miss Jeanette Lovell, a local girl, was also an old girl and she taught us English after Miss Veronica Darby, an English woman, was shocked to realize that we in Antigua actually spoke English and were not cannibals hanging from trees. Miss Mary Hood taught us geography. Mrs. Ruth McDonald taught us history, and Miss Rosemary Goodwin, another old girl, was one of our math teachers, while Miss Hyacinth Walling, yet another old girl, taught us French. She was followed by Miss Muriel George, a more mature and very strict French teacher who was an old girl of an earlier period. Miss Veronica Evanson, another old girl, was our first Latin teacher, to be followed by Mrs. Winifred F. V. Cooke, who was followed by Mrs. Gertrude Spencer. Another old girl was Mrs. Kathleen Flax, who was our home economics teacher; Mrs. Leola Roberts was the biology teacher;

Mrs. Vivian Starnes was our art teacher, and later, Madame Ledou taught us French very briefly, and then she was followed by Monsieur Mulloin, a French Canadian. He and Mr. Clarvis Joseph, our history teacher, were the only male teachers we encountered at the Antigua Girls High School.

Every morning when the first bell rang we assembled in our classrooms to take attendance. When the second bell rang we filed into the auditorium, form by form, with the sixth formers at the back, then the fifth formers, then the fourth, then third, second, with the first formers at the front of the auditorium. The elementary section of the school was under the supervision of Miss Bennett and Miss Coates, two English ladies. During assembly we would sing a hymn from the *Anglican Hymn Book*; Miss Blake would read the scripture or have the assigned student read it; and then we would kneel on the floor to pray. Instead of closing our eyes, some of us would look at the soles of girls' shoes. This was when we discovered that some of the girls in front of us had cardboard in their shoes for soles. Miss Blake would then read the announcements of the day and at the end we would return to our classes with lady-like decorum.

At the Antigua Girls High School the girls were trained to assume leadership positions. In each class the students elected a class monitor who would represent the class and assist the teachers during class time. Then there were school prefects who were chosen from fifth and sixth forms. During the GCE exams when the prefects were occupied with testing, prefects were selected from the fourth form to deputize in the interim. Then at the top of the rung was the head girl. She was the head honcho. The prefects and head girl had real power. I realized that when I deputized as a fourth former and then later when I became a prefect. We performed gate duties. When the first bell rang all girls were supposed to head to their classrooms, but that was not always the case; thus, the prefects went to the gate—which would then be closed—and let in the late comers whose names would be written in the log, and those girls would be given detentions, supervised by the prefects. We also had to be sure that girls wore school uniform at all times, especially the Panama hat each girl was required to wear, which some girls refused to wear because they alleged it destroyed their hairdos.

The school's *Prospectus* clearly outlined the school's rules, and one of them was that we should not be seen wandering the streets of St. John's in our school uniforms. Parents were instructed not to require their daughters to run errands for them. We girls were always amazed when Miss Helen or Miss Mamie complained that we were not the kinds of well-behaved students they were as students because we knew we were angels. Years later when I started to teach in Antigua and heard girls chatting loudly in public while wearing the school uniform wandering the streets of St. John's, without their Panama hats, I understood what Miss Helen and Miss Mamie meant. I even wondered what they would have thought, but they had been spared such an encounter.

I thoroughly enjoyed my five years at the Antigua Girls High School, especially the years I worked with Miss Helen as the first student librarian, which gave me access to large numbers of books, as many as my book bag could hold on the weekends.

After Mrs. Roberts, our biology teacher, left the island, we joined the biology class at the Antigua Grammar School, taught by Mr. Lambert, but that experiment was short-lived. We were more advanced than the young men and we complained that we were being held back. The School Board found Miss Smythe to become our biology teacher. It was she who prepared us for the overseas examination, the ordinary level of the General Certificate of Education (GCE) 'O' Level.

Chapter 7

The Domestic Front

In Antigua we were told that education was the way to upward mobility. Our parents may have had the basic education, some leaving school in various elementary grades to assist their families by entering the work force, but they wanted us to have the opportunities they did not have. Many parents sacrificed much to ensure a secondary education for their children. Unfortunately, some of the girls would soon follow the footsteps of their mothers by becoming unwed mothers, repeating the cycle. Not all girls fell in that trap. Some actually fell in love, got married, and started their families. In Cedar Grove there were no apartments for rent. At times a house may have become available if the owner died, but that happened infrequently because houses were very scarce. The process of falling in love and getting married was not as simple as it seems to be today. If a young man was seen too often alone with a young lady word would spread around the village that they were going together. This could pose problems for them both from their families, so the appropriate thing was for the young man to approach the young lady's father, who would interrogate him. In some cases the young man had to write to the girl's father or mother. One very important question was his intentions toward the young lady. He would then be asked about his financial status and his ability to provide for a wife and a family. Often times the father was not married to the young lady's mother, but that courtesy was still extended.

When a couple decided to get married the young man would build a two-room house, consisting of a bedroom and the other room for living and dining. He would construct an outhouse and a kitchen outside. Later, as their finances increased and their family grew, he would add more rooms until the house would in no way resemble the original structure. Building in Antigua today has improved to the extent that most of the houses are unique in architecture, with many rooms. I sometimes wonder who cleans such huge houses.

Even though many of our parents lacked a secondary education, they valued education and tried very hard to encourage us to continue our education. Many of them could not help their children, but they were very inventive. They would always identify someone in the community such as a teacher or a minister, who would help us with our work. We would start taking "lessons" after school and during the weekends. The payment for these lessons was very creative. It could be in the form of services, such as cleaning the teacher or minister's house, laundering the clothes, preparing meals, or even providing ground provisions or a chicken.

Our parents were not paragons of virtue, but they held us to very high moral standards. They expected us to avoid their misfortunes by maintaining high moral standards. They were very strict disciplinarians who believed that if they spared, "the rod they would spoil the child." That was taken literally. All children in our village were disciplined with the strap or the switch. This was a deterrent for some of us, but there were those children who seemed bent on the path of destruction. Darling raised us well. She resorted to proverbs when words failed her. If she received complaints about us hanging out with the children of questionable reputations, she would repeat the accusation to us without bothering to verify its accuracy, but she would conclude with the proverb, "Birds of a feather flock together." There was nothing we could have said that could have changed her mind. She doubted our ability to influence our friends positively, remarking that, "When you lie with dogs, you rise with fleas."

If the parent network learned of a girl's unmarried pregnancy we would be bombarded with a plethora of sayings, "What is done under cover of darkness will be made clear in the light of day." When the young lady complained, she would be reminded, "When you make your bed, you have to lie in it." Some of the more attractive girls in the village were arrogant and thought they were superior to others. Such girls were called "scianze," and that had nothing to do with the subject of science. If such girls were to fall and the "fall" could mean only one thing—pregnancy—we would be reminded that, "Pride goes before a fall, and a haughty

The Domestic Front

look before destruction." Darling seemed to have a proverb for every situation.

Education in Antigua relied very much on memorization. I always wondered why my mother knew so many proverbs and excerpts from poems and books. When we thought the demands placed on us were stringent, Darling would quote:

> *Lives of great men reached and kept*
> *Were not attained by sudden flight,*
> *But they, while their companions slept,*
> *Were toiling upward in the night.*

Henry Wadsworth Longfellow must have been a favorite of theirs. We heard constantly the following words:

> *Tell me not in mournful numbers*
> *Life is but an empty dream.*
> *But the soul is dead that slumbers*
> *And things are not what they seem.*
> *Life is real, life is earnest*
> *And the grave is not the goal*
> *'Dust thou art to dust returnest'*
> *Was not spoken of the soul.*

That poem would ultimately end with the famous words:

> *Lives of great men all remind us*
> *We must make our lives sublime*
> *And departing, leave behind us*
> *Footsteps on the sands of time.*

We often did not understand the words at first, but they were so greatly imprinted on our memories that we thought about them unconsciously, and eventually they started to make sense. My mother was a very humble person. She was kind to a fault. Many villagers would send for her when they needed assistance with the birth of a child, a sick person, or even to lay out a dead person. She also assisted financially. There was a certain family who conveyed the impression that they were superior to us in the village. They lived on one of the estates, but they lived way above their means. That was not because of laziness, but more to extravagance. Many times, especially on Friday evenings, one of the sons would show up at our house with the message that his mother would like Darling to lend her the grocery money so that they could buy food. I wondered what we would have eaten when Darling gave her the money. They always got the money, and we never went hungry.

My mother taught us humility by her life and by her proverbs. Her favorite saying was, "She stoops to conquer." I thought that was a Darling original until I encountered Oliver Goldsmith much later. Of course we could not understand the logic of that saying. How could anyone conquer by stooping? But her life satisfied our questionings. She manifested an easy disposition to the point that some people thought that she was too submissive, but she taught us to be strong individuals, strong women. To this day I repeat that saying on many occasions, especially when I am challenged by others who think they have full control. My mother's stance taught me that the one who shouts the loudest doesn't necessarily have the answer, nor does that individual have the power. She taught us that, "a soft answer turns away wrath."

Cedar Grovians were a clannish people to some extent. That could have been attributed to the fact that most of us were related. We could count the few strangers who lived among us on one hand, and they blended in so well that we did not think of them as strangers. One such blended Antiguan was Mr. Wade, a Dominican who had married a Cedar Grovian and moved to the village. His home was a frequent place for us to visit because his daughter Muriel was our friend and they kept her on tight reins. We on the other hand were allowed to wander freely around the village, so when Muriel couldn't come out to play, we would go to their home. Both Mr. and Mrs. Wade spoke French Creole, also known as patois, so often we would hear them conversing and we would pretend we understood when we really didn't. We affectionately called them Madame and Moucher Wade, which was our corruption of "Monsieur." Moucher Wade played the banjo. Many times he would play and sing for us and we would sing along until it was time for us to go to our homes.

The Domestic Front

Harriette Hickson, affectionately known as Het, lived with the Wades. Her mother Narna Boatswain of Montserrat was a good friend of the Wades. She was older than Muriel and was the friend of my older sisters. One day, after I had won the island scholarship to the Antigua Girls High School, I was running through the village bare footed, as most children did, when Het called me and gave me a pair of black loafers and said, "Now that you'll be going to High School, you can't walk around barefooted." My status had changed without my realizing it. Other adults in the village encouraged me. Mrs. Paige, Madame Wade's sister, called me Miss High School, and even many years later after I had left High School and college and was a teacher, she still referred to me as "Miss High School." I had brought honor to my family and by extension to my village by winning the island scholarship. They were all proud of me and encouraged me along the way.

Chapter 8

A Ride Anyone?

Cedar Grove was the only village in Antigua that did not have regular bus service. It was alleged that we refused to pay the bus fares, but I believed it was because we had such a close relationship with the wealthy residents of Hodges Bay, who would pick us up and drive us into town. Another reason could have been that we were only four and a half miles from St. John's, which we could have walked to in an hour. There were a few Cedar Grovians who had cars who offered to transport us as well. Every school morning the road from Cedar Grove to St. John's would be dotted with people, primarily students in uniform, who were on their way to school. I often chose not to walk in groups because sometimes those who would stop to pick us up could not accommodate groups. On rainy days my father would take us to school and even pick us up in the afternoons, but many times his job with Shell and Texaco required him to be all over the island, sometimes too far away from St. John's. I did not mind walking home from school because I read along the way. If no one picked me up I would read the whole way home.

I was very concerned in the morning because I hated to arrive at school late. As a result of this, my parents arranged with Mr. Joseph at Royal's Estate to take me into town in the morning. I would walk from our house to the corner of Royal Pond Road where Mr. Joseph would stop and pick me up on his way to work. For the five years I attended the Antigua Girls High School I was never late and I never missed a day. I sprained my ankle once and had to walk with crutches. My brother Wilmouth drove me to and from school every day until I was able to walk without the crutches. Often, I was the first girl at school, soon to be joined by the Abbott sisters who arrived on the Sugar Factory bus. Julie, Blondel, Sheila, Heather, Sandra, Brenda, and I would always be there to welcome the other girls as they trickled in by car or on foot. The other Abbott daughter, Sonia,

A Ride Anyone?

boarded in town with the Georges most of the time, so she would attend later with Eva Mae Harris.

Many of us country girls who attended school in St. John's ate at the homes of relatives or friends of our parents. When Mave, Hazel and I attended Girls School we ate our lunch at Darling's friend's home. Miss Cotty was my mother's age and they seemed to have been friends for a long time. She welcomed us into her home that she shared with her son Roy. By the time we would walk from Girls School on the outskirts of St. John's to St. John's Street where Miss Cotty lived, we had just enough time to bolt down the lunch we had brought from Cedar Grove, clean ourselves and the kitchen up, and rush back through town to school. At the end of the school day we would walk all the way from South Street to Hyman Village where there was a bridge, which was a favorite spot for Cedar Grovians to wait for a ride home. Because Darling always warned us about the ills of loving too much company—"By your company you shall be known"—we would leave our friends at the bridge and walk on. Sometimes we would stand a little distance from the bridge. At other times we would start walking home until we got a ride or walked all the way home. We sure did a lot of walking. No one could accuse us of being obese.

When we stopped eating at Miss Cotty's home, I started eating at our cousin Mave Francis's home on Long Street, where her nephews and niece—Ralph, Maxwell, Anthony, and Claudia Francis—also ate. When Mave cooked she fed us all, and when Darling prepared ducoona and salt fish, pepper pot, and other cultural dishes, she would send some for Mave. Mave also gave us juice or soda, so we didn't have to buy anything to drink. She treated us very well. Her daughter Valerie moved to New York to complete her high school education, so we became the children to whom she catered, but she accommodated us well.

When I did not take a prepared lunch, I received thirty cents, which would buy me two meat patties and a cupcake at The Nook on St. Mary's Street. The proprietor, Mr. Joseph, ran a tight ship. His wife and children, along with a few helpers, including Delta, attended to the growing lunch hour crowd, so that we did not have to wait very long to be served. Mr. Joseph was the bookkeeper and supervisor. With his sharp pointed pencils, he recorded every purchase, noting the food ordered and the prices paid. Paying thirty cents for lunch may seem very insignificant, but Mr. Joseph made a fortune from his restaurant. One of the sayings that hung around the restaurant remains with me today, "A man without a smiling face should never open a business." Mr. Joseph insisted that his waiters and his son Conrad accord us the best service no matter how small our purchase was. When Mave visited New York, at lunch time I would walk to The Nook, make my purchase, and select a table. At such a meal I would order a soda or a milk shake. I was always glad that I walked back to school to burn off the effects of such a scrumptious meal!

While we worked the lands we also kept cows that we got milk from. After my brothers had milked the cows we would scald the milk in a big pot until it boiled, and then we would take it off the fire and let it cool. My experience in being assigned to watch the milk so that it would not boil over into the fire proved the truth of the saying, "A watched pot never boils." I would watch the pot of hot milk and it didn't seem to do anything, but as soon as I took my eyes off the pot, voila, the milk would be at the top of the pot running down the sides into the coal fire. I hated the waste of good milk and the possibility of the milk putting out the fire. That would mean that we would have to relight the coals to continue cooking the breakfast, which was usually cornmeal porridge or rice porridge.

After the milk had boiled we would take it off the coal pot and put it on a table. We would then skim the cream off the top and eat to our heart's content. Every Sunday I would take two bottles of milk to Mave in St. John's. I would ride a bicycle with the two bottles carefully wrapped in newspaper to avoid breakage. I liked riding in St. John's on Sunday because all the stores were closed and traffic was nonexistent. It was as if everyone had decided to stay home and give the vehicles a rest. The challenging place for me was Teego Hill, where I walked up most of the time, but I enjoyed speeding down Friar's Hill without applying brakes. Then I rode the long stretch of road we called Lang Pa, for Long Road, which ended at the St. John's Cemetery. From the cemetery I would ride along Hyman Village Bridge into town; then I would ride down Newgate Street, turn left at Corn Alley, and then turn right on Long Street. The ride back

A Ride Anyone?

was uneventful and I walked up Friar's Hill Road then sped down Teego Hill. Sometimes I would stop to pick dumps, small green fruits, growing on trees at the top of Friar's Hill or other fruits that grew on the sides of the road.

Chapter 9

Local Fruits

Cedar Grove was the only village that did not seem to grow any fruits of significance. Most of the fruits in Antigua were grown on the southern part of the island, especially in Old Road. In Cedar Grove we had many tamarind trees, so we ate the green baby tamarinds that we called chickie. We ate partially ripe green tamarinds that we called flourie and we ate the dry tamarinds as well. Some of our friends always seemed to know where the sweet tamarinds grew and we would barter, beg, or buy them from the measly cents we had accumulated. Sometimes we would lay the dry tamarind in brown sugar, roll it, and make tamarind balls, or we would stew the tamarind and make tamarind jam. We did not make tamarind drink, which has become very popular in the past few years. Sometimes we would pick buckets of dry tamarinds, shell them, and sell them to Mr. Fernandez in town to make soap.

There were so many creative ways to earn money. We couldn't expect allowances from our parents because they could not afford such luxuries. Every tamarind season we would repeat a popular tamarind story. Millie Jonas and Sam were our neighbors, living to the west of us. They were the grandparents of Velma, Hyacinth, Icilma, Violet, Vernon, Glenn, Jas and Basil, our cousins Alister, Bobby, and Henley whom we called Mr. Kerr. It was alleged that Millie and Sam went to pick tamarinds once and Sam saw some lovely tamarinds perched high on a thin branch at the top of the tree. He boasted that he would get them. Millie was very concerned because the branch was very high and even though Sam was a very small wiry man, Millie was afraid he would fall. When Sam insisted that he would climb to the top to get the tamarinds, Millie said, "Sam, if you climb up dat tree and you farl dong, me go laugh."

Sam replied, "Millie, if you laugh, you na get a sprig."

Local Fruits

Besides tamarinds, dumps grew all around the village. Sometimes they would grow on the sides of the roads, but often they were on people's properties behind fences. We always knew when they were blooming by the stench that issued from the flowers, but that did not deter us. The dumps behind fenced properties were challenges for us, especially when dogs were tied right under the dump trees or around the yard. One of the sweetest dump trees grew in Miss Baby's yard. Miss Baby and Mr. Ernest Anthony, also known as Ernest Iron, cohabited after Mrs. Anthony moved to England where she lived for many years. Miss Baby was not a Cedar Grovian; she came from Bethesda and lived with Mr. Anthony. She and Mr. Anthony would sell the dumps, which people bought because they were big, juicy, and sweet. Miss Baby was my mother's friend and sometimes I had to run errands to their home. For my service they would invite me to pick some dumps that I didn't have to pay for. I liked the ripe yellow dumps and the brown snotty ones. Even after Mr. Anthony died, Miss Baby continued providing us with dumps. In the pre-TSA days, when I visited Antigua, I would get bags of dumps that I would take to St. Croix and enjoy eating them there.

Another popular fruit in Cedar Grove was the paw paw, locally called poopa, and also known as papaya. That is a versatile fruit. When it is green we boil it, cool the water, and drink it to control high blood pressure. We would mash the boiled fruit and serve it with salt fish and eggplant, or we would include it in our pepperpot. If any of the fruits survived to ripeness we would eat it anytime. Much later, when I lived with Aunt Gertie, when the ripe papaya was not sweet she would add ice cream to it. This made it taste much better. We really didn't care too much whether the fruits were sweet or sour. Of course we preferred them sweet, but, "beggars weren't choosers," so we ate anything we got.

Much of the fruits and provisions sold in Antigua arrived by boat from Dominica. On the days when the Dominica boat arrived at the wharf near the St. John's Market, hucksters would congregate to buy their week's supplies and then they would sell them in the market or in their villages. Several women from Cedar Grove were among those hucksters. One of them was Aunt Annie. I don't think she was originally from Cedar Grove, but she was very friendly with Gladys Weekes and her family. Aunt Annie lived at Tapa Hill, a little way from our home at Barnes House. She and my mother became friends and she became one of Hazel's two godmothers, so we all called her Aunt Annie. She had no children, but one day a young lady named Fernie showed up and she stayed with Aunt Annie until she produced Sonny, whom she left with Aunt Annie when she left Antigua.

Aunt Annie had a donkey on which she had a donkey cart, the only one in the village. Each side of the cart was laden with fruits and provisions, which she sold to her customers. She would walk with the donkey from Cedar Grove to Hodges Bay, all the way to the Antigua Beach Hotel, stopping at the homes along the way to sell her fruits and produce. After she had made her final stop, she would walk back to Cedar Grove and set up her produce on the steps of Gladys Weekes' shop. After we inherited Uncle Willie's house we lived very close to the Peters and Weekes.. We would run errands for Aunt Annie in exchange for some of the not too wholesome fruits, but again, we welcomed them. Beggars could not be choosers.

During the summer Darling would get the seller's bug and join the hucksters who met the Dominican boat. She started selling mangoes and other fruits, everything we loved, but we were well disciplined children and we did not have to be told twice that we could not eat the profit. We gladly enjoyed the soft mangoes, bananas, and anything that Darling couldn't sell. Sometimes when we returned home from school for lunch all we would eat would be mangoes or other fruits. Our breakfast of cornmeal porridge, which we called carnmeal pap, may have filled our stomachs because we didn't have great cravings or hunger pangs. Our big meal was at dinner, which was often served very late. This was understandable because we would return home from the grounds by sunset, then we would have to light the fire in the coal pot and get the meal going. Sometimes we would collect wood along the way to start the fire. Most often we would sit around the glowing coal pot and tell stories while we awaited our dinner.

One of the popular fireside stories was about the lizard that was cooked in the dinner. One woman was cooking her family's dinner by coal pot in the back yard. The pot was uncovered, and when it was finished cooking the mother served her family and they sat on the steps and on the stones in the yard eating their dinner. One child exclaimed, "I got the fish head!"

Another child exclaimed, "I got one of the thighs, which is very sweet, even though it is so small. Did you cook the little chicken, Mama?"

Mama looked at her children with a puzzled air. "Me na put non meakine in de pat. Me meen too weary fu catch and kill and pick de chickin, so me just put de provisions in de pat with the seasoning. Me wanda if one lizard jump in de pat when me nineda look? Wha na kill fatten." ("I didn't put any meat in the pot. I was too tired to chase and kill and then pick the chicken, so I just put the provisions in the pot with the seasonings. I wonder of a lizard jumped in the pot when I was not looking? What doesn't kill will fatten.")

Eating late had its advantages. After we would eat, those of us assigned to do the dishes would wash them in the dish pan that we had filled with the water we had collected earlier from the tank. Because we did not have running water in our homes, we kept water barrels that collected rain water. During the dry seasons we would transport buckets of water from the tank on our heads until we had filled the barrels. The tank was a great spot for socializing. Darling seemed to have timed us from home to the tank and back, so if we happened to stay longer than we should she would be after us. As soon as she turned Mr. Roseau's corner someone would whisper rather loudly, "Darling!" That was enough to send us scampering. We always met her before she got to our friends because we knew her very well and we didn't want to be embarrassed in public. She was one woman who had no shame when it came to disciplining her children. You would think that we would be more compliant knowing whom we had to deal with, but I guess that's the nature of the beast.

Chapter 10

The Sea All Around Us

Some children then, as now, were very creative, which proves the truth of the saying, "Necessity is the mother of invention." The Steven boys, Ferdie, Alcott, Henson, and Leon constructed a cart that they put a whole water barrel on. Of course when they started filling their water barrel those of us with our buckets gladly waited, enjoying the time to socialize. Then when we got home and Darling questioned us about how long it had taken us to get the water, we would complain that those boys for Power and Nurse Stevens kept us waiting while they filled their barrel. Of course Mr. Stevens and Nurse heard of that and got the truth. The tank is on the road leading from Cedar Grove to Hodges Bay. Some of us had to walk up Punty Hill, to the top of the street, and then walk to the northern part of the village where the tank was. When the Steven boys were carting their barrel of water, they would walk up Punty Hill pushing their cart with an empty barrel, but after it was filled they pulled it down the hill. I guess it was more pulling than pushing because if they had pushed they would have lost control and spilled the whole barrel of water. Our house was on Punty Hill at that time. We had outgrown Uncle Willie's house, so we were happy when our parents decided to resume construction on a property they had bought some time earlier.

The house was a huge two-story concrete structure that had once been worked on, but the work had stopped. For years it was left untended, so bush grew in it and animals occupied it. The goats were the most possessive, claiming their territory with their mounds of droppings, to the extent that the property was called the Goat Hotel. We moved into the house during my first year at Antigua Girls High School. We would peek through the glass windows to watch the Steven boys as they attempted to keep the filled water barrel from toppling over into the gutter. We couldn't watch them from the steps because we were supposed to be busy and if we were caught watching them we would be accused of being idle and, "Idleness is the devil's workshop."

During those days we worked hard. We were always busy because there were always chores to be done. Not having electricity and other amenities such as running water required more time to complete simple tasks such as bathing. We would fill the galvanized bath with water and bathe; then we would throw out the water so that someone else could bathe. That simply meant that we did not get full baths every day. Sometimes we would bathe in the back yard, using a pail with water, and we would pour the water over our bodies. We took many half baths during those days. We would bathe the essential parts in the morning and evening; then on Sundays we would have full baths. During those days we went to the beach very frequently and we would bury our bodies in the sand then wash it off. We took hygiene very seriously then, primarily because we could not afford the perfumed soaps and lotions.

The sea was one of our favorite places, and our parents seemed not to mind when we went. The closest beach to Cedar Grove was Royal Bay, in Hodges Bay. During those days no one had any right to claim the sea or to block entrance to the sea. The fishermen anchored their small fishing boats at Royal Bay and when they returned with their catch people were often waiting for them. Sometimes they did not wait until the fishermen got to the village because by then the choicest fish would have been sold. At that time a pound of fish was twenty-five cents, and a pound seemed much more than it does today. During the school holidays we spent a lot of time at the beach. After a few hours in the ground, we would rush to the beach where we would luxuriate, but that was not the sole purpose of going to the beach.

Sea grapes were a favorite among us all. At that time we did not eat imported fruits because they were not available, so we lived on the local fruits that we found. Since no one claimed the beach front, the sea grapes were available to all of us. We would head to the beach armed with our pails or buckets, which we would fill with purple juicy sea grapes. We ate so many that our tongues turned purple. We also collected whelks, the shelled creatures that live on the rocks. Sometimes we would get our pails full and when we got home Darling would cook them and we would have whelks and rice or stewed whelks, or we would just extricate them from their shells and pop them into our mouths. Another favorite from the sea was the cockle. Easter was the best time to dig cockles. Armed with our pails and buckets we would pull up the old pants that we were wearing. We couldn't afford bathing suits so we swam in old pants and T-shirts. We would assume the posture of one on a mission, with one foot in front, ready for action and the other behind for support. We would then dig our heels into the sand until we felt a hard object. We would bend over, extricate the cockle from the sand, place it in a bag around the waist, and continue until the bag was full.

We would then go to the shore, empty our bags into the buckets, and go back to continue our task. Sometimes the hard matter may not be a cockle, but a stone or even a cockle shell filled with sand. That did not deter our efforts. The mouth-watering taste of cockle and rice was adequate incentive for us.

We ate practically everything that the sea produced. Because fish were very common we ate them often. We contributed by helping the fishermen pull their fishing boats onto the land because they always gave us the little fish they chose not to sell. My father and his brothers were hobby fishermen who caught lobsters, eels, octopi, conchs, sharks, fish, and anything else the sea produced. The lobsters were often cooked right away. The eels and octopi were usually corned and then cooked. Because we had no refrigerator, excess fish, meat, eels, octopus, and anything that had to be kept was corned. After my mother and older siblings had cleaned them they would cut them in several areas and pour lots of sea salt into the cuts. Then they would place the corned meat on the roof of the shed, which could have been used for the kitchen. On the roof the sun would cure them and dry them. We were very careful not to leave them over night or in the rain. As soon as there were indications of imminent showers someone would run to the shed with a large container and collect all the corned meat. If they got wet they could develop maggots and we would have to throw them away or re-salt them. Throwing them away would have been a great loss, so we often cleaned out the maggots and re-salted them, beginning the process all over.

Cleaning the conch was another matter. After getting the animal out of the conch shell my parents would pour cornmeal on it to remove the slime. They would then pound it with a stone until it was soft. That was supposed to make it cook much quicker, since we did not have pressure cookers. After the conch was cooked my mother would stew it, curry it, or make conch souse.

Another favorite of the Knowles clan was eating crabs. All our homes had barrels filled with crabs. My father and my brothers would go crab hunting. We knew that the mangroves housed the crabs. When it rained heavily their holes would get flooded and they would walk out looking for dry holes. Sometimes they walked out under the cover of darkness and my father and brothers would be waiting for them with their flambeaux and crocus bags. Once they got home they would put the crabs in the barrels where they would purge them before they could cook them. Purging entailed starving them for a few days then feeding them cooked cornmeal fungi without okras or salt. After the recommended time the very active crabs would be placed in oil can of boiling water where they would be cooked over a robust fire. The crabs like the lobsters had to be placed live in the hot water.

After they were cooked my father would begin eating. My mother would have cooked a pot of okra fungi while the crabs were being cooked. Papa would take the legs off, crack them, and eat the meat. He would then pull off the back, take a lump of fungi into his fingers, and dip it into the crab back.

The turtle was another favorite dish. In addition to turtle eggs, which we enjoyed before they became endangered, the green gooey turtle meat made a sticky turtle soup. The turtle would be cut out of its shell and then cut up into manageable portions that would be cooked. Even though the animal was dead its flesh jumped throughout the cooking, but by the time it arrived on the table it was fully subdued.

With all the creatures produced in the sea, our meals were rich and varied. Of course we raised fowls, goats, sheep, pigs, and cows, one of which was always slaughtered at Christmas. The meat would be sold to neighbors, but the head, feet, heart, liver, lungs, kidneys, and entrails were reserved for us. The head and feet were cleaned of all hair and wool and then cut up. When the head was split open the brains were secured for the brains cake that Darling made later. The rest of the head and the legs were used to make souse. The heart and liver were reserved for Sunday breakfast, while the entrails were cleaned of all waste. That was a delicate job because while we wanted to get rid of all the waste, we did not want to puncture the entrails, which would be scalded and reserved for the rice pudding.

When the animal was slaughtered the blood was collected in a bowl and set aside. A little salt was added so that it would not coagulate. Darling would cook a huge pot of rice that she would mix with the blood of the animal and other seasonings. Then with the assistance of a selected stick that she would have had one of the older siblings strip of its bark and clean, she would stuff the rice and blood mixture into the entrails. When they were all stuffed she would put them in an oil can of boiling water to cook. After they were cooked she would take them out of the water, put some sweet oil (cooking oil) on them, and they would be ready to be sold. Rice pudding, also called blood pudding, to distinguish between the rice pudding made of sweetened rice, was a favorite among Antiguans. People from St. John's and other villages would reserve theirs and pick them up that day. The male reproductive organ was cured, stretched, and later used as a lethal weapon when wielded with the intent and strength of an angry, bloodthirsty person. No part of the animal was wasted.

Chapter 11

Indoctrination of Moral Principles

Being raised in the fifties and sixties had its benefits as well as its setbacks. We worked very hard because our parents took their responsibility of raising us to be exemplary citizens very seriously. They believed that they were entrusted with the task of raising God-fearing children who were to be well equipped to assume their roles in the larger community. They knew that idle hands were the devil's workhouses and so they worked hard at beating the devil in the fight for their children. To counteract that, they kept us occupied at all times. There was no occasion for us to sleep late because our mother's policy was, "Early to bed and early to rise/ Make a man healthy and wealthy and wise." To prove how wealthy and wise we were, Darling would remind us that, "The early birds catch the worms."

Of course, "worms" was the metaphor for opportunities and other benefits that our sluggish friends and neighbors missed. We must have been tired and sleepy some of those mornings when the alarm and not even the rooster that seemed to lodge outside our window could wake us, but our dear mother who awoke us reminded us that we should, "rise and shine."

She would always insist that we have our devotion to express our gratitude to God for His "saving grace." My mother did not have the opportunity to pursue an education, but she applied what she learned. She had heard or read that we should always be reverent in God's presence, even when we worshipped at home. Reverence included not only our deportment, which was excellent because we were very subdued, being heavily intoxicated with sleep, and anxious for the opportunities to snooze while someone read the scripture and someone else prayed. So there was no problem relating to reverence in our deportment. We were to be appropriately dressed, which meant that we had to don our regular clothing in place of our sleepwear. Darling believed sleepwear lured us back to sleep and so she insisted that we change into outside clothes as soon as we got out of bed. The final criterion was a little more difficult and sometimes created some humor among us. All females had to have our heads covered. We neither dared nor approached the Creator with uncovered heads, so we would show up in all manner of hats that were readily available. In the absence of the hats we would grab a towel, a sheet, or even a blanket that would not only conceal our heads, but our whole bodies. That made it very easy for us to fall asleep. Many times we would be interrupted rudely by a nudge from a sibling inviting us to participate in the worship.

The family worship was not the only time we submitted our plans and our lives to God during the day. That was the first time. At school, we also had morning assembly, which was the devotional activity for the whole school family. At the St. James School, later named the Cedar Grove Elementary School, the morning ritual was the same Monday to Friday. When the bell rang we would line up in front of the school with our backs to the crèche and the St. James Anglican Church. The teachers would inspect our clothes. At that time there was no uniform policy, so we wore our school clothes to show the distinction between our home clothes and our church clothes. The school clothes were a little better than our home clothes, which were our demoted school clothes, and the school clothes were the demoted church clothes. That progression in itself presented us as a medley, with some students wearing regular clothes while some girls wore lovely dresses, somewhat worn, with bare feet.

The school inspection included our whole bodies. We would stretch out our hands so that the inspecting teacher, always accompanied by the strap or a ruler, could examine our nails and fingers. I always found it so unfair because some of us had to complete manual labor before we went to school and it was not always possible to clean our nails of the dirt and grass. So even though we would bathe our nails were not always clean. For dirty hands we would be punished with a few licks from the strap or the ruler.

Next would be our hair. I don't know if they were searching for lice, but they often found bedbugs. Many of us were intimately acquainted with the little bedbugs that slept with us, sucking our blood, and forcing us to soil our bed clothes by crushing them between our fingers and the sheets, which would then receive their foul blood. I don't know if bedwetting was hereditary or whether so many of us were experiencing psychological trauma, but many of us were habitual bed-wetters. We knew who the bedwetters were because our parents seemed to inflict the same punishment on us. Our punishment was to wash the bedclothes that we had urinated in and hang them on the line to dry. Sometimes we would try to delude our parents by getting up out of the wetness, changing our night gowns, and hiding them and the bedclothes under the bed. Of course that lasted only a short time because the rankness of concealed urine would soon expose us and we had to pull them out, head to the bathtub, and start laundering. That would also retard our progress, and when we arrived late to school we had to expose ourselves by telling the teacher we had wet our beds and had to wash the bed clothes.

Many of the home remedies proposed to stop bedwetting were applied in our home as well, but the ones I recall were to limit liquid intake to 6:00 p.m. daily. We were forced to use the bathroom before we retired for the night and Darling would even arouse us at strategic times so that we would use the appropriate disposal system instead of the bed. Some other herbal remedies, which I have forgotten, were applied, but I believe the sempervivum, our single bible, was somehow implicated. We used that plant for all ailments and proposed ailments, internally and externally. It is not surprising that the aloe vera, our single bible plant, has assumed such a prominent place among herbal and practical plants. We were bribed, threatened, and punished physically, but those last resorts seemed ineffective. When our bodies or our maturity level was ready, it helped us to hold our urine until the morning, or it forced us to get up during the night to relieve ourselves.

I don't think some of the parents understood the motivation or the fear factor that kept us snuggly in our beds and beddings before, during, and after the act. In our house many of us shared a bedroom and one bed, which meant that some of us had to sleep on the floor. We loved sleeping on the floor because it meant that we didn't have to make the bed the following morning. The thing that we liked most was that when we slept under the bed, we were protected from danger, which was always perceived as jumbies or spirits of the dead. We had heard many stories about dead people appearing to the living and we felt that their intent would always be evil. We concluded that if any spirit entered our house it would have to encounter those on the bed first and somehow we would be protected in the fray. The other thing that lured us to the floor was the fact that we could hide under the bed to evade wakeup calls and even chores, although that did not happen. However, the best thing of all was the companionship and potential scapegoats who would sleep with us.

The older siblings had earned the rights to the bed, so we were consigned to the floor. Each night we would collect our beddings, roll them out under the bed, and after we had prayed we would slip in and snuggle up in our beddings. We didn't mind being crowded because it meant more security. I was the primary bed wetter. I would recall the great desire to empty my bladder and somehow it was always shrouded in a dream where I would dream that I got out of bed, went to the bathroom or the utensil/chamber pot, familiarly known as the "po," and relieve myself. While enjoying that great relief, I would experience a warmth that enveloped my body; then I would feel very cold. It would be at that time that I would awake from dreaming and reality would tell me that I had wet the bedding.

Very quickly and quietly, I would sneakily crawl out from under the bed, change my night gown, and hide it somewhere. I would then sneak back under the bed, climb over my heavily sleeping sister, and push her into the wet beddings. In the morning I would deny all accusations, claiming that my nightie was dry. But then one smart sister would produce my urine soaked nightie rolled up and hidden somewhere in the house.

Fear was a great producer of wet beds. Many of us had outhouses or latrines, which meant that any attempt at relieving ourselves would require our getting out of bed, going outside in the dark, and into the dark outhouse where all kinds of rodents and spiders resided. However, our greatest fear was being caught by jumbies. We had heard enough about the doings of creatures from the spirit world and we knew that we would prefer to face our mother's wrath the following morning than be embraced in the cold arms of a wandering spirit. Sometimes Darling kept a white enamel chamber pot that we fondly called the "po." We would use

Indoctrination of Moral Principles

the "po" during the night, put it away carefully, and wait until the morning when someone was assigned to empty it, wash it, and turn it down to dry until it would be placed into service during the next night. The septic replaced the chamber pot, and with the convenience only a room away, which could be illuminated by the flick of a switch, our fear of the dark gradually disappeared and with it our bed wetting.

While I don't remember the exact date when I stopped wetting the bed, I do know that it ended before I entered high school. I also knew that some of our classmates had similar problems because their parents were less diligent than ours. Those classmates did not bathe as frequently as they should have, so sometimes their body odors and rank-smelling clothing gave them away. At that time the Health Department engaged on a campaign to rid Antigua of bedbugs and lice. The convergence of several initiatives seemed to work. In our home Ros migrated to England, which created bed space for us. We were therefore promoted to the bed, which required us to get rid of our beddings. The bed wetting ceased and some sense of respectability was returned to our homes and to our village.

Chapter 12

Communal Activities and Student Bonding

After the inspection of our persons was completed to the teachers' satisfaction we would have our morning prayers outside. We lined up according to our classes, with the infant class in the front and the most senior students at the back. We would sing a hymn from the *Anglican Hymn Book*, the headmaster would read a passage from the Bible, and we would repeat the Lord's Prayer. That pattern varied. We sometimes marched into the church after inspection, sat in the pews by our classes, had morning prayers, and then launched into rehearsal for our school's cantata. Later, when Alister Francis was the headmaster, after inspection we would go to our classes, stand in place until the morning prayers were over, and then sit and commence the day's activities.

At 12:00 p.m., when the bell rang, we would put away our work, stand and repeat our Grace before Meals—"For what we are about to receive, may the Lord make us truly thankful, Amen"—then we would rush home to whatever fare awaited us. Sometimes it was only bread and butter with limeade, affectionately called brebitch. We would run an errand or two; then head back down the hill to get in a few minutes of play before the bell rang to resume afternoon classes.

In our classes we would stand, clasp our hands, and close our eyes as we repeated Grace after Meals—"For what we have received, may the Lord make us truly thankful, Amen." At the end of the day we would sing another hymn and repeat the evening prayer. Our days were filled with a routine of prayer that reinforced the divine presence in our lives. Our parents and our teachers reminded us of our allegiance to God and we lived accordingly.

Communal Activities and Student Bonding

I spent one year at the St. John's Girls School, where Mrs. Vivian Lake was the headmistress. Mrs. Lake was a stalwart of a woman, tall, well endowed, and of prominent deportment. Morning worship at the St. John's Girls School required us to stand in our classes, in our seats behind our desks. We would sing a hymn and every day repeat Psalm 46: "God is our refuge and strength, a very pleasant help in time of trouble." We would get that far when Mrs. Lake's resounding voice would call us to halt and remind us that, "God is always pleasant; the psalm does not say 'pleasant,' it says that, "God is a very present help in time of trouble." So we would begin the psalm again, noting the psalmist's words accurately. Mrs. Lake was an excellent example to us in all things, especially in her ability to clearly enunciate and pronounce her words.

At the Antigua Girls High School, a private school with an auditorium, we would assemble in classes as we sang the morning hymn, listened to the reading of the scriptures, and knelt on the floor to pray. Our graces before and after meals were repeated in individual classes, and we were dismissed at the end of the day by the teachers in the last classes.

I liked Thursday mornings at the Antigua Girls High School. Even though it was a private school when I entered Form I, The Antigua Girls High School had been a parochial school, under the auspices of the Anglican Church, so it retained some of the trappings of its parochial past. On Thursday mornings all Anglican students would cross the street to the St. John's Cathedral where a sister would conduct confirmation class. A Methodist sister and a Catholic sister conducted such classes in classrooms on campus with the Methodist and Catholic students respectively. All other students met in the auditorium. I don't know what transpired initially because as an Anglican I would cross the street and work with Sister Winifred as we prepared for confirmation by learning the catechism. A few years later when I became a Seventh-day Adventist I joined the group downstairs, and after a while we conscripted Janice Nibbs, my classmate, into service. She was one of my classmates who was a Moravian. She played the piano and we sang for that whole period. Some of the songs were as follows: "There's a Tavern in the Town," "In the Gloaming," "Maggie," "Clementine," "Frere Jacques," and "Row,

Row, Row Your Boat." I don't recall being supervised, but I remember those days and the fun time we had singing those good old songs. The spirit of community was ever present, and we felt our social, spiritual, and educational needs were met.

Chapter 13

Security and Stability

Socially we were well endowed, even though we did not have televisions, shopping centers, malls, or any of the mega amusement media where children wander at will with friends so that they can experience life and life's treasures. We did not know that we were living in a third world country, nor did we know that we were deprived. We had good parents who loved us, even though they did not express their love in the heavy emotions we see today. They showed their love by being excellent role models for us, by teaching us sound moral values, by exposing us to the spiritual tenets of our lives, by keeping us busy at all times, and by feeding and protecting us. They may not have built us huge mansions, but they taught us the value of gratitude and contentment, and they emphasized the importance of cleanliness, for, "Cleanliness is next to Godliness."

Our parents did not have to prove their love by overwhelming us with toys and gadgets. The occasions that required gifts, such as our birthdays, Christmas, and major events such as confirmation, were occasions for practical gifts. Because money was scarce, gifts had to be planned in advance. That sometimes meant that at harvest time when we reaped the fields, sold the produce, and received the bonus, all the gifts would be bought and concealed.

Our gifts were usually school supplies—like books, pencils, or pens—clothing, shoes, or a doll that Darling had made for one of us girls, or a piece of tool or a cart for the boys. We have even received calves born to our cows as personal gifts. One such animal was Allan, a bull calf born to one of our heifers. I think Allan was given to Ros, my oldest sister, but he became everyone's pet. We became so attached to him that when he was to be slaughtered we put up strong opposition. However, that did not stop the show because we were very practical children and we knew that the money from the meat would have been invested wisely by our parents. We also knew that we would have eaten well off the various products of Allan that had not been sold. We learned very early that there was a great difference between reality and wishes. Hadn't we learned the words of one poem that said, "If wishes were horses, beggars would ride"?

Since there were five daughters in succession in my family, after three sons, Darling would buy bolts of fabric, which was much cheaper than buying the fabric by the yard. She would then make a dress for each one of us and one for herself. The beauty of this was that when she wore her birthday dress in January we girls knew that each one of us would get a dress of the same fabric, even though it may not be the same style. My birthday was next, in March, so I would be very surprised when my new dress was revealed. Ros would receive hers in April, Hazel in June, Mave in October, and P in December. We may all have decided to dress similarly for church, but that was not usually the case. Of course we also wore hand-me-down clothes that our older siblings had outgrown. Sometimes Darling would literally remake the clothes, but other times we grew into them. We younger ones were the recipients of the hand-me-downs, while Ros and P often got new clothes.

At Christmas, our home, as were the homes of our neighbors, was decked out in festive colors. We would begin by putting all the furniture on the porch and literally cleaning the house from top to bottom. We had to extricate the cobwebs from the roof, wash the windowpanes, and clean the glass windows until they shone with newspapers reserved for the occasion.. After scrubbing the floor, a feat that could have been accomplished only on our knees, we dried it with the appropriate rags, and while we allowed the moisture to evaporate we dusted and polished the furniture. We had a huge mahogany dining table, mahogany Morris chairs, and a mahogany center table in the living room. O Cedar polish was the only polish we knew would do justice to our furniture. We would also wash the cushion covers, starch, iron, and replace them, giving the chairs and the house a new look.

Additionally we would take our best china wares and glasses from the cabinet and wash them as well. I always wondered why we bothered to wash them because they were never used and they were enclosed behind glass in the cabinet, but Darling required them washed so we had to comply. As we grew older and more hands were contributing to the family income, we started buying appliances that we could not have afforded before.

After we had cleaned the whole house we would replace the old linoleum on the floor with a new one and then bring in the furniture and create that Christmas look. We often decorated, but we could not afford real Christmas trees so we would use imitations. We would also get new oilskin tablecloth for the table. After all this we would begin the real meaningful part of Christmas, which was the cooking. Those early days saw us eating everything, without discriminating. We would boil the Christmas ham, bake a chicken or two, and of course we would have the fresh meat from the animal we had slaughtered. Darling would bake the Christmas black cake and bread. She was an excellent cook and she knew how to feed a large family as thriftily as possible. Growing most of the produce did help to a great extent. Our maternal grandmother, Aunt Alice, was also an excellent cook and baker. We all liked her doving pot, which produced some of the most delicious gravies.

Papa would buy the drinks, especially our favorite liqueur: falernum. That would be added to the homemade sorrel drink, ginger beer, maubi, and anything else my mother decided to make. While the food was for the family, we knew that friends and neighbors would stop by anytime during the Christmas/New Year's celebration, and it was traditionally appropriate for us to offer them something to eat and drink. Some of our guests boasted that they had left their home before breakfast that morning and had been fed at all the homes they visited. I then wondered what happened when other neighbors decided to visit their homes!

Christmas was never the same without us singing Christmas carols. We would plan to visit the neighbors' homes and serenade them with the most beautiful songs that reappeared each Christmas. Shoul's Chief Store distributed books of carols that we prized dearly. We would end our singing with the following saying, "Christmas is a coming, and the goose is getting fat/ Please to put a penny in the old man's hat. If not a penny, a half penny would do,/ If not a half penny, then God bless you." That was an example of our love of oratory, but it elicited goodies from the hosts and some members of the family would join us as we went to other homes where the routine would be repeated. By the end of the evening our numbers would have swollen significantly and we were the recipients of bottles of homemade drinks, black cakes, and all other kinds of goodies. We shared the loot and went to our separate homes.

Sometimes we would sing at the hospital and share the loot with the less fortunate. Disposable containers were not popular, so we kept washing the glasses and the dishes that had been used so that we could reuse them as guests kept dropping in. Our homes were open to all. At no time do I recall my parents or any neighbors asking who someone was. Our neighbors' friends and relatives were just as welcome as they were and all guests were treated courteously and hospitably. On some occasions those who had over-imbibed curled up and slept and we allowed them to sleep off the effects of the alcohol.

Chapter 14

Typical Caribbean Furniture

I remember when we got our first refrigerator. Before that acquisition we kept our food in a poor relation of the china cabinet called the safe. The safe was constructed in a similar manner to the china cabinet, but it was less ornate and instead of the glass at the sides and on the door there was gauze, which allowed us to see its contents, but kept out the insects and rodents. Sometimes the ants waged war with us and creativity intervened. We would get four round empty butter cans, fill them with water, and place the legs of the safe in the water. That way the ants could not get in. Of course we would be sure to remove the safe from touching the walls of the kitchen in order to thwart the ants' plans. Whoever denied that, "necessity is the mother of invention?" It's amazing that our leftover food would be kept well in the safe until the following day when we would heat it up.

There were some meals that were always better eaten the following day. Some of those were pepper pot, rice, fungi, and dumplings. Pepper pot and rice were simply heated, but for the fungi and dumplings we created wonders. Darling and my sisters had developed the skill of cooking fungi by boiling the okras in lots of salted water. When the okras were soft they would pour some of the water with the okras in a bowl and then pour the cornmeal in the water remaining in the pot on the fire. Using the turn stick, they would turn the meal and the okras until the okras were mashed, creating a yellow mush with green particles. They would keep adding the okra water until the fungi was the right consistency. Then they would add some butter and turn the fungi while turning off the fire.

In a buttered bowl, they would spoon balls of fungi until there were enough balls for all of us, with the older members receiving larger balls of fungi. The fungi pot would then be filled with water, so by the time we would finish eating we could scoop the residue out of the pot and wash it with the dishes. Fungi is such a versatile dish that we would eat it dropped in the pepper pot, or with stewed fish, or with salt fish and mashed eggplants and spinach, or with stewed smoke herring, or with stewed liver or any other stewed meat. I have never mastered the skill of turning fungi a la my mother and siblings, so my fungi cooking requires me to soak the cornmeal in water and then to pour the wet mass into the boiling water. In doing this I am able to control it and eliminate the lumps.

One favorite way of eating fungi was when it was one day old. A ball of fungi would be placed in a covered bowl in the safe. The following morning it would be sliced very thinly and fried crisp in hot oil. We would then eat it alone, with butter, or with cheese, and that would be breakfast. Today that favorite dish is known as polenta, popularized by the Italians.

The other dish that we enjoyed the second day was boiled dumplings. Those would be relegated to the safe, where they would lodge until the following morning when they would be sliced and fried. Boiled fried dumplings were another favorite breakfast meal that we enjoyed. Often our breakfast strayed from the typical breakfast fare, but we rationalized that we were hard workers and we had to eat meals that would give us the stamina to perform our duties. Sunday was the only day when we could predict our breakfast. Its only variation was liver when we had slaughtered an animal. At other times the salt fish breakfast reigned supreme.

One of the Knowles traditions was that we should be fed according to the work we produced. It may have been an incentive to generate work out of us, but it was also a sure way of developing gluttony. That was manifested throughout the year, but more so during cotton picking time. I was the youngest actively involved child on Papa's property at Powell's Estate. I don't know if my small hands and body gave me an advantage over the other siblings and adults, but I filled my flour sack tied around my waist many times, rushed to the large burlap sack where I emptied my cotton, and went back and filled up again and again. I must have been a highly competitive child, but I was awarded an adult's meal because I worked hard. While the incentive was a positive one, it caused me to eat more than I really should have and that led to serious problems with obesity.

Typical Caribbean Furniture

In our family food was a metaphor for love. We fed those we loved our choicest foods in copious measures. That could have been descended from our Grandmother Jane Ann Knowles. She was always in the kitchen and she always had a meal for anyone who stopped by. While my experiences with my grandmother were limited, I seem to have very fond memories of a generous, loving woman. However, as I heard her stories being recounted by relatives and complete strangers, I understood and believed because I saw replications of those experiences in her daughter, my Aunt Gertie.

Aunt Gertie left Antigua when she was eighteen-years-old and travelled to New York where she lived for forty-six years. On her infrequent visits to Antigua, we would travel to the Cove where Grandpa had taken up residence to see our aunt who was visiting from New York. Aunt Gertie was a tall, well-endowed woman, a specimen of the Knowles tribe. She always brought things for us. In those days clothes from America were highly valued. It didn't matter that some of them were hand-me-downs or what we now call used clothing. The point was they were new to us. In Antigua we called such clothes waggee. We would envy our friends who had relatives away, which was any place away from Antigua. Some were in England, Canada, America, or even other Caribbean islands. The important thing was that they would prepare boxes or barrels of food and clothing that they would ship to us in Antigua. When the boxes or barrels arrived our mothers would unpack them, parcel out the contents so that each child would receive a gift, and then distribute food and clothing among the neighbors. Of course there were neighbors who would accept gifts from our barrels, but when they received their barrels we knew of it only when we saw them wearing new clothes that did not look like the clothes made or bought in Antigua.

When Aunt Gertie retired and returned to Antigua I lived at her home and saw her thoughtful consideration of not only her neighbors, but her hospitality to the police who were stationed at Fort James. Her policy was very simple. The police were there to protect her, as well as the other residents, and the least she could do was to offer them goodies such as cakes, tarts, and biscuits that she baked weekly. Thursday afternoons were her outings. She would pack a basket of goodies, dress in her Sunday best, and I would drive her to the country where she would buy fresh eggs and produce from the vendors. At each stop she would present a package of cake, bread, tarts, or anything she had baked. This became our Thursday ritual. As time went on she invited her friend Mrs. Anita Edwards and her neighbor Mr. Alfred Smith to come with her. My Datsun B210 would be filled with a hilarious group of seniors who were going on their trip to the country, equipped with baked goodies for friends.

On various occasions when Aunt Gertie and I sat on the porch after dinner and after cleaning up the kitchen, she would recall snippets of the past, dropping a hint here or there. She talked of her life growing up as a female in a home dominated by men. She and her mother, my grandmother, the only females in the great house at Powell's Estate, would cater to the men— Grandpa and her five brothers—who worked from sunrise to sunset each day. Sixteen years later her sister Molly was born, but in three years Aunt Gertie was shipped off to New York.

I had heard different versions of that trip, but never from Aunt Gertie. Some of the bits that slipped out were enough to allow me to put things together and I arrived at a version that I consider the truth. Aunt Gertie was a very tall, strapping girl, just entering her teen years when an overseer from a neighboring estate started to look at her knowingly. Mr. D, himself a handsome gentleman, thought marriage to the older daughter of George Knowles would have enhanced his position, but Gandpa had other ideas. When it was rumored that Gertie Knowles was seen at a certain estate, Grandpa made her reservations on the next ship traveling to New York, bought her ticket, and Gertie found herself packed and boarding the vessel. In 1921 the trip to New York took about a month and Gertie soon found herself working in the great metropolis that would become her home for forty-six years. Experiences of her New York life became the subjects at our evening sessions on the porch as we observed the people traveling to and from the Fort James beach, where they soaked their bodies and luxuriated in the warm refreshing waters.

One evening we relocated to Aunt Gertie's bedroom where she was sorting through her trunk. She took out a box of letters, looked at the greeting cards yellowed with age, and shook her head; then she said:

During the war, we recycled paper, but we didn't call it that then. When we received greeting cards, we would cut them apart, and use the paper for grocery lists, to write letters, or even to write recipes. We would then use the pictures to decorate our room or to make gift books and gift boxes. Now, many years after the war, I'm still holding on to the greeting cards. Old habits are surely hard to die.

On another occasion, when we were looking at the photo album with all the black and white pictures of people in the strangest looking clothes, Aunt Gertie introduced me to all the children who had passed through her care during the years she worked as the dietitian and cook at the school. I became acquainted with many pictures, but there was one picture that she consistently passed over. Each time I saw the picture I became more curious, but I was told not to question adults; I had to show respect. I waited for a long time and then one evening when she took out the album I knew the time had come. As we looked at pictures and she told me the stories of the people she finally came to the handsome gentleman.

"Aunt Gertie," I said. "Who is this handsome white man?"

She paused, and then asked: "Which white man?"

I pointed at the picture and she said, "Oh, him, that's Sal. Salvatore Rogusa. He was my husband."

I sputtered. It was a good thing I wasn't eating because I would have choked myself. She continued, "I see you are surprised. Sal and I were married, but it didn't last."

I looked at the tall handsome man. I wasn't surprised because Aunt Gertie was a tall woman, 6'1" in her stockinged feet. However, something gnawed at my sensibilities. She must have sensed it, because she continued:

Salvatore Rogusa was an Italian American. We thought we were in love so we got married, but Sal was too jealous. He was handsome, generous, and funny, but he was too jealous and too possessive. Every day I had to give an account of the day's activities; I couldn't go anywhere without his permission, and I had to account for every penny I spent.

She paused, as if to catch her breath after such a long statement; then continued with a faraway look in her eyes and a smile on her lips. "I loved Sal, and I think he loved me, in his way, but I had been on my own for too long. When I left Papa and Mama's house in Antigua at the age of eighteen, I lived on my own. I couldn't tolerate Sal's jealousy and his many questions. We had the marriage annulled, but we remained friends."

She stopped, and I asked, "Did Grandpa know you'd been married? Did your brothers know? Nobody ever said anything."

Aunt Gertie smiled and said, "There was no wedding; we were married by a justice of the peace, and I thought I would tell Papa and the others later. By that time Mama had died. Maybe if she was still alive I would have told her, but Papa and my brothers were busy with their lives, and your Aunt Molly was also immersed in her children and her collection of husbands. The marriage didn't last, so there was nothing to tell anyone. You are the only person who knows that I was ever married."

The topic died there. It was never resurrected.

Before she retired Aunt Gertie visited Grandpa periodically, but as her retirement drew near she employed Uncle Oliver to build her a house. She had been sending practically every penny she made to Grandpa and he invested in Cove Head, buying choice real estate for Gertie. After he had divided Powell's Estate among his five sons and Aunt Molly, he built a house at the Cove and moved there to start developing Gertie's property. He landscaped it, planting fruit trees, erecting a cistern, and digging a well. He also cleared the land, which was ready for Aunt Gertie's house to the west of his house. As he sat on his porch, as he did most afternoons, he would be looking directly at Aunt Gertie's house.

As construction progressed her visits became more frequent and the trips to the shipping agent and the customs division were followed by truckloads of furniture, cooking utensils, and other furnishings. Retirement for my aunt meant the closing of the New York chapter and the opening of a new chapter at the Cove in Antigua. She was a lady and she planned to entertain like a lady. She hadn't spent forty-six years in New York working seven days a week and all holidays to grow old and die in Antigua. She had money, thanks to her father's thriftiness. In addition to that, her Social Security check would be coming every month and with the currency exchange of nearly five EC dollars to one US dollar she would be sitting real pretty.

Uncle Oliver completed the house a few months before Aunt Gertie retired. He had his men clean away the debris, cut the grass, which wasn't ready to be mown, and brought four truckloads of topsoil for the garden. He seemed to know just what she would have liked and he had everything ready for her.

For the first few months Aunt Gertie set up her house and started a garden. She planted pigeon peas, okras, sweet potatoes, spinach, and greens. She also planted roses and other blooming flowers in the front. Her brothers visited regularly, because they were visiting the, "old man," who was in his nineties and had slowed down significantly. They liked to visit Gertie however, because she was an excellent cook and they liked to eat her pepperpot, fungi, saltfish, and her chicken foot soup. They didn't care about steaks and such because Gertie's cooking reminded them of their mother's cooking.

Gertie liked having her brothers around and sometimes the wives and girlfriends visited, but she wanted to cultivate some friends of her own. At times when she thought about friends she wondered what her life would have been if she had not left Antigua. She started thinking of an occasion for a party and she thought a housewarming would be the perfect thing. She started thinking of the guests and began her list with the newly-appointed Governor, her cousin Sir Wilfred Jacobs and his family. As she thought of relatives and acquaintances, she realized that her list was growing considerably. It was time for her to pull out the cookbooks and start planning the menu. That was the easiest and best part. Then she wondered if she should get the real Baker's unsweetened chocolate for her scrumptious dessert and she started to make her shopping list.

Aunt Gertie was a planner; she prepared for all eventualities. A few days before the house warming she mentioned to the police officers that she would be expecting some friends at her housewarming and casually asked them to drop by if they could. Her casual invitation was an indirect request for them to police the area and keep the peace. Fort James was a popular tourist location and the beach lured many people to luxuriate in its refreshing water, so the road was highly trafficked. To eliminate traffic problems, Aunt Gertie had her guests drive into the yard and park on the spacious lawn.

They came in their coats and ties, senior citizens who still believed that any function away from home required formal attire. Aunt Gertie was dressed in her stocking and heels. In place of her hat, she chose her favorite wig, which looked very natural with gray hair interwoven between the black. She even wore her pearls. She was in her element. The food had been cooked and the spacious living room and dining room were set to accommodate the guests, with overflow on the porch where she had set tables with her white starched and ironed embroidered tablecloths. The fine crystals, chinaware, and silverware were set strategically. She even had a bartender. She had told me earlier that her friend Dennis was going to tend the bar because he was a mean man and she knew that he would dole out the alcoholic beverage carefully.

The hors d'oeuvres were deliberately sparse because Aunt Gertie didn't want her guests to be too full to do justice to her huge baked turkey, stuffed rock hind, vermicelli rice with caramelized potatoes, and tossed salad. Her Devil's chocolate cake was the piece de resistance. All of this was followed by coffee or tea.

The housewarming, an overwhelming success, was followed by tea at the Government House a few weeks later and a few invitations from some friends, but as the weeks rolled into months the invitations and telephone calls started to dwindle. Aunt Gertie realized she was spending more time at home than visiting other people's homes. The highlights of her life became the weekly Thursday trip to the country to buy home-grown eggs, fresh vegetables, and to get a bag of chicken legs. Aunt Gertie started to make a big event of that trip. On Wednesday she would bake her signature pound cake, coconut tarts, breads, and buns. She would parcel them out for the homes where we would stop and she would also reserve some for the police who were stationed at the Fort James Police Station. There would be no more parties or entertaining. She looked forward to her brothers' visits, with their large families, and to the visits of other relatives who knew they would always get something to eat at Cousin Gertie's home.

Chapter 15

Other Activities

Many of our social activities originated in history and were usually community oriented with involvement of the whole village. Besides the holidays surrounding Christmas, New Year, Easter, The Queen's Birthday, and Commonwealth Day, we also celebrated Guy Fawkes Day. Guy Fawkes was the infamous Englishman who plotted to blow up the British Parliament, but was caught before the deed was executed. On November 5, we would celebrate Guy Fawkes Day by burning worn tires, sometimes pulling the burning rubber through the streets of the village. Several children would be the victims of such conflagrations, but the celebration continued every year. The following morning we would clean up the particles of burnt tires, but the black patches would disappear over time.

We were primarily an agrarian community who worked the land from which we eked out a modest livelihood. We would prepare the soil by plowing, weeding, and building banks; then we would plant the seeds and wait for them to germinate. While we waited we kept weeding, which kept us busy all the time. Then as the plants grew we would thin them out for healthy growth and the weeding continued. We fought a constant battle with the grass and bush native to the areas we cultivated, but the devil grass seemed most persistent. Darling would advise us not to be content with chopping the head off the grass because its roots descended into the ground and created many sections. To get the whole root we would dig and pull until we got the whole root system. Many times we would reconstruct the banks as a result of our intent on eradicating the devil grass. But alas! In no time the devil grass would grow back and we would have to begin the eradication process all over again.

During the harvest we would reap bountifully, especially when the weather cooperated with our efforts. At the end of the harvest, after all the crops had been reaped and before we prepared the land for the next crops, we would celebrate harvest thanksgiving, which was a religious affair. We would select the choicest produce from the grounds and cart them off to the church where the committee would decorate the church with the long, thick, succulent sugar-canes, forming arches at the doors and windows of the church. The bunches of fruits and vegetables as well as the hands of bananas would be arranged aesthetically, with baskets of fruits and root vegetables as well as leafy green vegetables placed at the altar. Of course there were beautiful bouquets of flowers placed strategically around the church as well. The church was transformed into a veritable agriculture show, but that was the intent as we expressed our gratitude to the Creator.

The whole service was centered on the theme of giving thanks and we expressed such in the songs we sang well, "We ploughed the fields and scattered the good seed on the land/ But it was kept and watered by God's almighty hand. So thank the Lord, oh thank the Lord for all His mighty love."

At the end of the day baskets of fruits and vegetables were distributed to the shut-ins of the village. The rest of the produce would be sold to the parishioners and the money would be placed in the church's coffers.

Another activity that brought the community to observe our men at work was the moving of a house. Many of the houses built when I was a child were constructed of wood and were often relocated as lands became available or as people moved. The house would be placed on the flatbed of a truck and men would ride along to balance the house while some would use sticks to remove overhead electric wires. Sometimes houses were transported from Cedar Grove to New Winthorpes or Pigotts, or vice versa. Such long trips were executed by skillful drivers and devoted assistants. When the house was being moved from one location to another in the village the men would place it on barrels and manipulating the house on the barrels with planks of wood. They would roll the house to its intended location. Once there, they would elevate the house on four well-chosen rocks at the four corners, which would keep the house firm until a hurricane or some disaster would shift it from its precarious foundation.

Other Activities

I enjoyed observing the men as they engaged in the arduous task of moving a house. Very often alcoholic beverage would be served around to enhance their courage and camaraderie. Some men would be very particular about protecting their backs and so they would wear huge belts or tie a harness-like contraption around their shoulders to protect their backs. They would position themselves at the four corners of the house, in a Samson-like posture, slightly bent over, and one man would shout, "Ready! Steady! Lift!" In unison they would all raise the house from the ground and place it on the flatbed truck if it was going to another village or on the rollers for relocation to another part of the village.

The shouting, heaving, and shoving would continue for a while, with some choice expletives thrown in periodically. We would follow the movers as their unsolicited cheerleaders and would stay until the house was erected on its stone pillars and we saw the curtains flying in the windows. Life was very uncomplicated then and everyone was very neighborly.

Their assistance was always solicited and they were always available. In those days projects were communal affairs. When one family decided to build a house the decision would be discussed with the neighbors who would instruct on the materials needed and just how the work would proceed. We were always amazed at the skills and expertise of the men, and often the women, who had received the minimum education, but who could create blueprints for houses and construct them as any degreed architect or engineer could. Most of the men worked the land or engaged in other jobs, so the help extended to the neighbors was relegated to the weekends. What times those were!

The event would be marked by the slaughtering of an animal or large quantities of fish reserved for the occasion. The women would prepare sumptuous meals of goat water and rice and peas with stewed meat, lots of fried dumplings, and fried fish or cooked corned fish. These were dishes that filled bellies quickly and fed many people. It was not surprising that practically the whole village would show up to eat because that was how we were then. We children were the gofers, running errands, fetching water, cigarettes, and anything the adults felt we were able to do. We really earned our meal.

A tradition that was alleged to have originated in Africa was continued in the village. While the men undertook large tasks they would sing rounds and, the work progressed very late into the night. It was not surprising that during those days buildings were constructed, sugarcane cut and transported to the factory and so many other jobs got done without the owners paying for them. They would provide the food and the rum, which the workers would consume as they engaged in the work. The communal activities helped to bond us as a community and they saved us a lot of money that we really didn't have.

Chapter 16

Social Traditions

Many British traditions were passed on to us in the villages and we enjoyed them, not realizing that we were actually imitating the colonizers. One such tradition was tea. We were poor people who worked hard and who lived thriftily. We managed three meals a day, even though breakfast and lunch could have been bush tea and cornmeal pap followed by biscuit and butter or fruits in season for lunch. Dinner was the biggest meal of the day and was cooked and served after we had completed all chores that the available light allowed. Afternoon tea was out of the question. Many of the females worked as domestic servants in Hodges Bay and Crosbies in the homes of wealthy white people. They were always required to prepare and serve tea, so they knew what tea was, but they did not have the time nor the means to serve tea at their homes. Who would be the tea guests anyway? All their friends would have been working as well.

There was an invention of something known as a singing meeting, which was also called tea meetings. I always wondered why it was thus named since it did not involve singing and no tea was served. What I recall about the singing meeting is a sense of competition where men of oratory would compete against each other. They would travel from village to village and meet in union halls or school buildings where the villagers would gather to support them. These men would be dressed in their finest, some of which were often ill fitting hand-me-downs. The suits would have seen better days and they could have been adjusted to fit the wearers, but that seemed not to be of consequence. The warriors, as they named themselves, were clad in suits with ties and that was very important. They were well suited down.

The meeting would begin when a loud voice would be heard at the back or coming from one of the side doors of the building. The warrior would announce his presence in highfaluting oratory, often times filled with malapropisms. "Here enters the valiant warrior from Freetown, auspiciously penetrating your presence to declare the declaration of the muses as I elucidate and educate yo, with no desire to entertain, but should that occur, blame not the speaker but the occasion." He would continue in such terms that he would obfuscate his meaning, creating much hilarity. Not only were they trained in elocution, but their performance was quite exciting. Sometimes the organizers would add humor to the occasion by laying wagers on the speakers. Some would place an amount to have them shut up and sit down, while someone else would place a higher bid to have the speakers continue. This would go on well into the night while the organizers collected a handy purse from the bidding.

At the end of the session after all the contestants had spoken, a poll would be taken to judge the best speaker. That was another matter of hilarity. The speakers were not judged only on their gift of elocution, but on their apparel, their messages, and their ability to entertain the audience. Sometimes favoritism would result in a biased decision that would end up in fights. The judges' decision may have been final, but it did not prevent the audience from expressing their disagreements vociferously. I think that was enhanced by the intoxication of those who had imbibed copiously of the alcoholic beverage. Tea could have been served at some time during the tea meetings, but that was replaced by alcohol, which seemed to add a special dimension to the session.

Chapter 17

Burial of the Dead

Paying last respects to the dead and assisting the families of the dead were duties that were taken very seriously. When I was growing up most of the people who died were old people. We did not have vehicular accidents because vehicles were very few, owned only by wealthy people who treasured them. We were very wary of them, so we stayed away from them. Today I will drive down Market Street in St. John's and pedestrians dare me to proceed because they refuse to move out of the way of oncoming traffic. Also, because cars are so very popular the congestion of traffic and impatience of drivers tend to result in major accidents that have proven to be fatal. The funerals that we attended in Cedar Grove were those of older people who had lived their lives and passed on. There were a few middle aged people who also died, like my Aunt Fernie, but they had passed forty.

There were two of our classmates who died young. The whole school and village turned out for the funerals. I remember when Goldine Barnes died. She was a tall, strapping girl, who had a heavy voice. Goldine was the daughter of Vio Kelsick, and she was the sister of Dulcie, Sonny, and Howard. There seemed to have been a health problem, but we did not know what it was. All we did know is that she had died and that her death generated great fear in us children. The funeral was very painful to us because she was one of our kind, but we were afraid that her spirit, her jumbie, would haunt us. We had played with her, been teased by her, and we considered her a bully, so we were afraid that her jumbie would be just as bad as she was. It was a very sad funeral.

The other teenager who died was Dave Belle. I don't recall his funeral, but it would have been held at the Gracefield Moravian Church since they were Moravians. Goldine's funeral was held at the Anglican Church. Dave had not been a well-child. His growth had been stunted and he was often sick. When he finally died we were not very surprised, but we were sad because he was a very friendly boy.

Before the funeral had been elevated to the stature it demands today, those who died were cleaned, dressed, and laid out in their living rooms on a dead board and people would pay their respects there. Before the funeral, however, there would be a wake. The wake was the village's way of comforting and supporting the family of the deceased. Neighbors would contribute crackers, bread, alcohol, and whatever food they had. After they had completed their day's chores, they would head to the home of the deceased where many people would congregate to comfort the bereaved. Sometimes the house was so small that the mourners would gather in the yard and tell stories, jokes, play dominoes, or just get drunk and go to sleep. Some people would stay through the night, which forced some hosts to stay awake. The principle was that the spirit of the dead was to be feared, and so the belief was that the more people there were in the house, the safer it would be for the family. Often relatives would fall asleep and leave their guests talking, playing, and eating.

There was no refrigeration to store the dead, so they were usually buried the day after they had died. If they died at home they would be laid out with the help of villagers who were adept at such things. The following day or two after, when the funeral would occur, the body would be placed in a plain coffin, taken from the house on the shoulders of the pall bearers, and would travel to the church by the longest route. No short cuts were taken at that time. As the funeral procession passed down the streets we would close our windows in respect of the dead, something that I never understood. Later, when the Barnes Funeral Home commenced its funeral services, the hearse would drive slowly from the deceased's home to the church, avoiding short cuts and taking the most circuitous route, with the mourners walking behind the hearse in procession.

After the funeral many villagers returned to the home of the relatives to support them. This could continue for a few days, or as long as the rum lasted.

Chapter 18

Other Eccentricities

What's in a name? Everyone has a name that may have been chosen for a family member, for a famous person, or simply because somebody liked it. There are nicknames or pet names that have been appended to individuals. Diminutive or shortened versions of people's names have suggested endearments such as Bob or Rob, or Robbie for Robert, Bill or Willie for William, and P or Penny for Penelope. Some people have completely different names. For example, Genevieve may be called Hazel because her mother saw the name in a book and liked it, but Genevieve had already been given her quota of three names, so she was affectionately called Hazel.

In early history, a person's name was their identification and addresses. Names could comprise their given names, their professions, their fathers' or mothers' names, physical traits or defects, and even the names of their homes. That was appropriate because people were defined by their places of residence. Linguaphiles claimed that, "the place of origin often turned into a generic term for some personal characteristics." Some examples of names of places being associated with a particular quality are, "laconic," which means using few words, from Laconia in ancient Greece and, "bohemia," which means unconventional, from Bohemia in the Czech Republic.

One of the things that distinguished us Cedar Grovians from many other Antiguans was our love of nicknames. Everybody had a nickname or a pet name. In each family there were names that were associated with family members' characteristics, behavioral patterns, or with physical handicaps such as shortness, tallness, fatness, or thinness. Even one's impaired vision could be the reason for the name Four Eyes. In the context of the family, or among friends, nicknames may symbolize a form of acceptance, but they were often coined through ridicule. The term "nickname" was derived from Old English in about 1440, from the 1303 word "ekename." An "eke name," when taken literally means, "an additional name." In Viking societies nicknames were used in addition to or instead of their family names. Giving nicknames was a ceremonious occasion that often resulted in the establishment of a relationship between the one who gives the nickname and the recipient of the nickname. During the ceremony gifts were sometimes exchanged.

Just about everyone in the village had a pet name or a nickname. In my family, Wilmouth was Willas, Ferdie was Dummy, Everette was Heads, Roslind was Ros, Violet was Penelope, also called P. Maviene was Mave, Genevieve was Hazel, I was Half Pound, George was Jubba, Franklyn was I Frank, and Annabelle was Bellas.

A nickname was meant to be a term of endearment and the bearer of the name responded to it amicably. Such nicknames as Dassa Sprat, Buckaroo, Quesequanda, Dadda Joe, Meat Head, Popee, Potogee, Barba, and Shorty may not sound very endearing, but through the years they have helped to create bonds that have survived the test of time.

One mother summarized the advantages of nicknames when she introduced her son as "Royie, short for Roy." Nicknames were meant to be shortened versions of people's names, names by which they were recognized and affectionately identified.

Nicknames can be categorized by physical deficiencies or abnormalities, by professions, character traits, or by associations. Some nicknames were derived from physical handicaps. My brother Ferdie was born deaf, which resulted in his loss of speech. People started referring to him as Dummy and that name stuck. We have never associated nicknames with any negative intentions because Ferdie has always been very popular and highly regarded by all. Nicknames may be philosophical as well. Someone who engages in philosophical discourses may be called Aristotle or Plato, which may be shortened to Aristo or Ari; he may even be called The Philosopher or Philly. One man in Antigua was nicknamed Studiation Brown because he argued that, "studiation is more productive than education."

When Miss Sophie was fitted with a wooden leg after her amputation, people referred to her as Half-a-foot Sophie, or Pegleg. I must admit that among us children we used the term derisively, but in her presence, or in the presence of other adults, she was Miss Sophie. Her nephew Keithly had an accident that left one leg longer than the other. When he walked the shorter leg required him to drop his hip lower. He was soon known as Hip-and-Drop Keithley.

Some nicknames originated from mistakes or mispronunciation. When the cartoon *Popeye* was introduced in Antigua one young man demonstrated Popeye's characteristics, flexing his muscles, attributing his prowess to his love of spinach, the miracle-working green vegetable in the can. He was soon known as Popeye. One other young man, who expressed an attraction for the sailor, referred to him as Popee. To this day the name has stuck. I don't think many people know that his name is actually Buel, not Popee!

People's idiosyncrasies are associated with their imitating movie stars or other historical figures for whom they expressed great attraction. Consequently, their behaviors earned them their nicknames. Their complexion was also contributed to their nicknames. My cousin Anita, whose father seemed to have been of Portuguese ancestry, is of a Portuguese complexion, which earned her the nickname Potogee, a creolized form of Portuguese. Her brother Fitzroy is called Bunksta, her other brother's nickname is Adam, while her youngest brother is Crucian. I cannot understand this because he has never visited St. Croix, nor is he affiliated with any Crucian, as far as I can tell.

One Cedar Grovian boy liked to yank. Yanking is the term used for speaking like an American or even an English person. Throughout Antigua and the Caribbean, we have distinctive accents that tend to identify our places of origin. Often, when people encountered American or English persons, they would attempt to adopt the American or English accent, be it mimicry or an attempt to impress the guests. These people would then be known as "American" or "English."

One person may have had several nicknames, which may be attributed to his/her versatility and popularity. One such person was my godmother's brother, whom she called Sarge, but who was also known as Punka, Buckaroo, and Barcroft. Then there was Noel, who was known as Kid Noel or

Noel the Kid. Another such character of many nicknames was my father. He was Miller, a name he acquired through his skills in the trade. He was also called Jubba, which was attributed to his resemblance to an ancestor by the same name. Later, when my brother George manifested a similar resemblance, he too was given the name. My father was cross-eyed, which made it very difficult for both eyes to look at anyone simultaneously; thus, he was called Cock-eyed Leonard. When any of his friends jokingly mentioned his cross eyes, he would smile and state, "I may see crooked, but I shoot straight."

Chicken Head was the nickname given to a young man whose small head resembled that of a chicken. Skinny was a thin boy who gained too much weight as a young adult, but the name stuck. Big Bobby gained his nickname through his corpulent size and imposing stance. As a child, Ole Man possessed the traits of a mature individual, and was affectionately called Old man, which morphed into Ole Man.

Some of the people whom I knew very well had some strange nicknames. Dassa Sprat, Rookoo, Buck Benny, Sugar Stick, Sebben, Likkle Jim, Boonooksie, Tallykin, Appin, Adam, Slim, Massay, Fundoo, Baby Joe, Heads, Windy, Blues, Winnie Ram Goat, Charles Derby, Sledge, Poopa, Miss Dean, Challee, Sacca, Duce, Chi Chi Whip, Marma Liz, Likkle Gal, Booda, and Busta.

Chapter 19

Methods of Discipline

Children in my generation were to, "be seen and not heard." We were taught our place and knew how to behave so that we would not embarrass our families. We hear much about the concept of shame among Chinese, but that had been very evident in our communities as well. We were always taught to respect our parents, other adults, and ourselves. Should our behavior embarrass our families, we would learn what it meant to bring disgrace on them. Not only were we punished, which was often a solid beating, but we would hear of it for the rest of our lives. Sometimes the spanking was more tolerable than the silences we encountered and the guilt that was inflicted on us. Those in themselves were great deterrents that kept us responsible and respectful.

The fact that the village was involved in raising us meant that we were literally responsible to the members of the village. That responsibility required us to respect them, to obey them, and to regard them in loco parentis. They had as much rights as our parents and we knew it. That concept helped to keep us in control of our emotions and our behaviors. It made us realize that our every action was being observed, and because we wanted to represent our families, we maintained our very best behaviors. Of course there were children who seemed unable to control their tempers and behaviors, and there were children whose parents expressed, in their presence, their aversion to other adults keeping check on their children, with the result that these children sometimes violated the code of conduct that we observed. Be that as it may, most of us knew that our parents would accept the community's version of any misdemeanor, so we walked that straight and narrow path.

When the village was given control of the children, we all benefited. We respected and obeyed the adults, whose all-seeing eyes and all-hearing ears were always vigilant to see us straying and to hear the expressions or conversations that we should not have been involved in. Thus, we were monitored on a daily basis, and that monitoring forced us to comply with the village's code. It was so very easy for us to detect violations because we knew the unwritten code that we had heard very often. It was the village's restatement of the Golden Rule. We practiced doing to others what we would expect them to do to us. It was so very simple.

On the other hand, when the village was allowed to exercise its parental rights, we the children benefited. Not only were we cared for emotionally, but we knew our physical needs would be met by the village. Often times parents in the village would take care of us just as they did their own children. We did not expect them to deny their children their daily needs, nor did we make demands on them, but the sense of community was a vibrant visible force. We were always told to leave our friends' homes at meal times, which we did, but often the parents would invite us to stay and share what little they had. The message being conveyed was as follows: If my children ate, you would eat as well. It was therefore not surprising when Darling would prepare a plate of food, bake a loaf of bread, or wrap some fried dumplings and ask one of us to take them to a neighbor. If our mothers—and it was always mothers—realized that we had been eating at a family's home quite frequently, they would compensate by sharing cooked food or produce from the ground. No demands were made; it was an unspoken policy that showed how astute our parents were in social relationships and the concept of reciprocity.

When the village is responsible for the children we all win. Our parents never had to pay babysitters and the Department of Child Welfare did not have to cite our parents for violations when they left us on our own at home. We were fortunate at our home because we had older siblings in the house, but when they were younger and the parents worked, they asked the neighbors to keep an eye on us. That eye was all encompassing. They would monitor our behaviors in the house, based primarily on the noise level issuing from the house. If it was too quiet, they would call out to find out what mischief we were engaged in. If it was noisy, they would remind us that children were to be seen and not heard. They would also check on us to see if we had food and if there was none they would provide it.

Methods of Discipline

Our maternal grandmother, Aunt Alice, and our aunts and uncles lived in the village with their families. We knew that they would have helped if we needed anything. Even though we knew that, we did not habitually make demands on them. We felt if our parents wanted their assistance they would have sought it, so we left such matters to the adults. Most of our older relatives, such as Dadda Maggie, our grandmother's sister, had grown children who lived on their own, but when Dadda cooked, she prepared enough for all the children in the yard. There were times when we would eat several dinners if we could time our visits right. When we showed up at meal time no one asked if we had eaten already. Neither were we asked if we would like some dinner. Another plate was filled and we would be served with the comment, "Your father must be a good rider because you showed up just in time for dinner." We would usually eat outside in the yard sitting on a rock or on a little bench.

The yard was a very popular place during my childhood. Most of the houses then were very small, with enough room to sleep and maybe a living room that doubled as a bedroom at nights. A room could have been built in the yard for the kitchen and the outhouse or latrine would be strategically located to avoid contamination of the air. There was no facility built for bathroom, dining room, or den. Those were luxuries that we could not afford. So the yard became the living room, dining room, bathroom, and kitchen. It's no wonder that one of our daily chores was to sweep the yard and make sure that it was immaculate to entertain our guests. In addition to the clothes heap—the huge pile of stones on which the white clothes were laid to bleach in the sun—each yard had fairly large rocks strategically positioned so that we could sit comfortably on them for social activities such as story-telling and eating. We children played a lot in the yard of whose ever home we were at. We knew too well that inside the house was not the place to play or run and hide, so we confined our activities to the yard.

There was a great distinction between the front of the house and the back yard. For those of us whose front doors faced the street, we would have steps leading up to the front door. Some neighbors had little porches that we called the gallery then. Later we replaced "gallery" with such terms as verandah and porch. We didn't have a gallery, but at Barnes House and later at Uncle Willie's house, we had steps leading to the front door. The steps were the place we would sit after the work was done and the sun had set, so there was enough shade and cool breeze to keep us comfortable. The steps were where the men would sit during cricket matches as they listened to the ball-by-ball play on the radio. During the day when the sun shone on the steps, the men would resort to the east window, which we would open so that they could listen to the game undisturbed. We would even provide cool water from the water jar.

Not having refrigerators, on very rare occasions, we would buy chunks of ice from the village shops, where the ice was kept in blocks in ice chests. In the absence of ice, we kept our drinking water in a clay water jar in an alcove built in the first room of the house. It was not the kitchen, nor was it the dining room, bur it served those purposes, as well as doubling up as a bedroom at nights. There was a dipper that we would dip into the clay jar to extricate the water, which we would pour into an enamel or tin cup. Glass wares were reserved for very special occasions when we had guests from out of town or even for local guests at Christmas. That water would taste so cool and refreshing that we never really longed for the ice cold water provided by the refrigerator. It's amazing how content we were with our lives, which we felt were full and very happy.

Chapter 20

Migration

Many of the people from the islands of the Caribbean knew that greater opportunities for upward mobility lay across the sea. Some Cedar Grovians were employed by the base when the Army and Navy arrived in Antigua as a strategic defense move to show their presence in the Caribbean. Fidel Castro had created quite a fuss in Cuba and so the United States felt it necessary to create a presence in a location from which they could move easily to intervene in problems. As a British colony, Antigua was defended by the British, but when the Americans arrived in the late 1950s it created problems we had not anticipated. Most of the soldiers were single men and some of the married ones had left their families in the United States. Therefore, it was not surprising,, when females from neighboring areas such as New Winthorpes, Barnes Hill, Pigotts, Cedar Grove, and other areas in Antigua, showed up at the base gate to display their wares and prostitute themselves. Some of the soldiers actually married Antiguan women, while others co-habited.

Both males and females were employed on the Base, where they had privileges such as shopping at the commissary and earning the Yankee dollar that was excellent exchange. Their standard of living was elevated. We saw this when they started building their houses and when some who already had houses added on bathrooms and kitchens. The servants were exposed to a different way of living and even though Cedar Grovians had worked as maids in Hodges Bay and Crosbies, and at the Beach Hotel and White Sands Hotel, they had been working for people from the British Isles such as England, Scotland, Wales, and Ireland, as well as those who had been born in Antigua of parents from Madeira and Syria. They seemed to have had good relationships, but the Americans were more open and shared a relationship with the maids that changed their interactions. There were also Black Yankee soldiers who won the hearts of many women.

American employers would drive their maids home and sometimes even pick them up so that they did not have to walk from Cedar Grove to the Base. Some even started visiting their maids' homes and sometimes they would leave their children in the village to play with the village children. When they returned to the United States for vacation some of them took their maids with them, and so Cedar Grovians were expanding their horizons.

Some of the young Antiguan men enlisted for the Army, which enabled them to become United States citizens, with all the rights and privileges pertaining thereto. That meant increased wages, possibilities for an education on the GI Bill, and unlimited opportunities. The horizons for many young people were opening up and they took advantage of all opportunities.

Some Antiguans started migrating to England, Canada, and the United States for job opportunities and to continue their education. The most enterprising ones started out as maids, lived thriftily, sent their money home, and were able to acquire property on which they built their homes in Antiguan that they returned to when they retired. Unfortunately, some regarded their migration as an opportunity to sever ties with their families on the islands. Two of my maternal grandmother's sisters, Aunt Florrie and Aunt Baby, migrated to the United States before I was born. I knew that they existed because their names were mentioned. They may have written at times, but they never visited. Aunt Baby, who was the younger of the two, actually died in New York. She and Aunt Florrie had married, but had no children. Years later, Aunt Florrie decided to return to Antigua and she stayed at our home since she had nowhere else to stay. She had a house built on the family property in Cedar Grove, west of where we had lived in Uncle Willie's house, and moved there when the construction ended.

From Aunt Florrie we learned that her sister, Aunt Baby, whose name was Beatrice, had been an accomplished musician. I even acquired some of her sheet music that Aunt Florrie had brought to Antigua in her trunk. Those ladies seemed to have forgotten their family in Cedar Grove, unlike other people who migrated to the United States and the United States Virgin Islands and sent for their children and other family members right away. The immigration situation was not as traumatic as it is now; so many people traveled on visitors' visas and later acquired green cards and then became naturalized citizens.

My paternal Aunt Gertie was one such individual who migrated to New York and later sent for her sister Aunt Molly, who later sent for her children. Aunt Gertie worked as a cook in wealthy homes, but her job, when she retired in 1967, was as a dietitian for a wealthy Jewish family. Aunt Gertie recounted that the family had a handicapped child and that they opened a school to accommodate their son and other handicapped children. Aunt Gertie planned their meals, cooked them, and worked with the family until she retired. She sent her money to her father, my grandfather, who invested in Cove Head where Aunt Gertie's house was built. She maintained connections by returning home periodically, communicating with her father and her brothers, and by investing in property. A few years before she retired her brother, Uncle Oliver, built her house and she relocated to Antigua.

Aunt Gertie shipped her household acquisitions, so when she arrived in Antigua her barrels had been cleared by her brothers and all her belongings were at her home. All she had to do was to unpack the barrels and set up her home. When that had been done she started a garden where she grew ornamental plants as well as tropical fruits and vegetables.

As Grandpa aged, his mobility declined and Aunt Gertie employed our cousin Margaret to live in the house and take care of him. I don't recall how Margaret was related, but she possessed the Knowles build and she was referred to as Cousin Margaret. Margaret was about 5'8", well endowed; tipping the scale at more than 200 pounds, and had a glossy dark complexion. She always reminded us that, "Black mahogany makes the best furniture," as she justified her complexion.

Margaret was not affiliated with any organized trade union. She had no written description of her job to my knowledge, but she never deviated from her schedule. She would prepare breakfast for herself and for Grandpa, then lunch, and dinner later. She washed about twice a week, and spent the rest of the time sitting on the porch. She must have cleaned the house, but it always looked the same to me—gloomy, with furniture in the same place, no rearranging, no attempt at beautifying, and no fresh flowers or bouquets.

After Aunt Gertie retired, she moved to her newly constructed house about 200 feet west of Grandpa's house. She planted flowers and vegetables and spent a lot time in her garden. As she looked over at Grandpa's house she would see Cousin Margaret on the porch, just sitting. Gertie thought she could help Margaret utilize her time and maybe make some money. She made her proposition thus, "Cousin Margaret, I can't get anyone to help in the garden even though people complain they can't get any work. Working the ground isn't what people want to do today." She got no response, so she ventured further, "Could you give me a hand in the garden now and then, after you have finished your duties, and have nothing to do?"

Cousin Margaret bolted up into an upright position, folded her arms over her corpulent bosom and declared, "Cousin Gertie, me may be big, black, and ugly, but me delicate." ("I may be big, black, and ugly, but I'm delicate.")

Aunt Gertie observed Margaret daily enjoying her morning and evening siestas, while she struggled with the devil grass and the bush that tried to reclaim her garden. Margaret stayed with Grandpa until he died in 1968, then she disappeared.

Another lady was a fixture at The Cove. She must have been named Jessie, but we called her Jessie Sea Louse. None of us children knew where she came from or who her relatives were. We didn't know if she was a member of the family. Whenever we visited Grandpa, Jessie showed up in her little house at the back. When she was not cooking her foul-smelling food, she would be fishing or digging for cockles. As I recall, Jessie was a frail woman who didn't say very much. I never saw her in conversation with either Grandpa or Cousin Margaret. I've never seen her in the house. She was always near the sea or in her little shed. The problem with her fishing, which may have led to our calling her Jessie Sea Louse, was that her diet consisted almost only of sea food, and there was a problem with that.

Grandpa's outhouse was built close to the sea. The constant washing of the waves to the shore must have eroded the ground on which the

Migration

outhouse stood because it was balanced precariously with the door on solid ground, but the back was conspicuously flushed by the sea water flowing in and out. Grandpa may have conformed to the building codes when he erected the latrine years ago. The standard procedure was a pit hole, about six feet deep, over which an outhouse was placed, with a commode that patrons would sit on. Some variations of the outhouse have been built as lavishly as the imagination or the pocket would permit; however, when we visited The Cove there was no pit hole, with the result that waste matter was deposited directly into the sea and then was washed away. Looking back at the situation, I can recall no concerns from environmentalists. I do know, however, that that was Jessie Sea Louse's favorite fishing hole. She fished daily, often covered up to her waist in water. When she had made her catch, she would climb up the bank with her soiled pail filled with an assortment of sea creatures—crabs, whelks, cockles, and fish—that had fed on the daily meal of excrement from Grandpa's outhouse. Thus, Jessie lived, no bother to anyone, on her daily diet. She disappeared before Grandpa died.

Chapter 21

Of Senior Care and Other Considerations

The village's responsibilities extended not only to the children, but to the senior citizens as well. There was an institution in Antigua for the indigent, but many residents thought it was highly unnecessary. We believed that families were duty-bound to take care of their members. The Fiennes Institute was the government's attempt at assisting those who were in no position to help themselves, but we firmly believed that our seniors, as well as all members of the village, were our responsibility. To this day I don't know of any Cedar Grovian who had been confined to the Fiennes Institute. Unlike some Europeans who built neighboring homes for their aging parents, we kept them in their homes and children and grandchildren attended to their needs. When they required around-the-clock care, we moved them into our best bedrooms and attended to them there. Our pride helped us think of what would be said of our aging relatives and we kept them in the best condition for visitors, doctors, and for the ministers who would visit to give communion or just to pray with them.

When my mother succumbed to leukemia at the age of seventy-five, Aunt Gertie said she heard about how well we cared for her, so much so that at no time did anyone who visited detect any foul smell or lack of care. She ended by saying, "That's how I'd like to go when my time comes."

On some occasions, senior citizens may not have had children of their own or their children may have migrated to other places across the sea. Villagers would become the care-takers of such individuals, attending to their personal needs, providing their meals, and cleaning the home. Those were not the days when people had to sign power of attorney, nor were there legal documentation. Later, when the situation became prevalent

Of Senior Care and Other Considerations   97

because of the longevity of seniors, offices were established to legally assign guardians of seniors. These guardians attended to all matters that the seniors were unable to attend to and they were paid handsomely for their services. Some of the guardians later became the owners of the properties and the seniors' money.

For us, money was not the incentive because there was none. We believed that life is a cycle and, "what goes around comes around." Our parents believed that they were demonstrating to their children what they wanted to be done to them. They felt it was their duty to attend to their parents and to the seniors in our village because they owed it to them to repay them for the services they had rendered. They taught us to respect and care for our seniors so that they would maintain the same quality of life they had enjoyed previously. They took great pride in knowing that they cared for their aging parents and neighbors to the end. When death occurred and the funeral was done modestly, there would be no guilty feelings or crocodile tears.

There have always been exceptions to all rules. There have been some children who neglected their parents, but God had always provided for such individuals through the church or through neighborly interventions. Then there were those who were never married, never had children, and even those who were not Cedar Grovians, but who had relocated there. One such person was Blind Tommy. Mr. Tommy Christopher lived at the northern end of Cedar Grove in Stevens, where he kept an immaculate yard and home. We visited daily because we were some of the children who ran errands for him. If my memory serves me correctly, I think he was once a military person who had lost his sight in combat. The point was that he was not a Cedar Grovian, but when he relocated there, the residents decided to take care of him. He had a monthly check that helped to cover his expenses. We were always amazed at the cleanliness and organization of his home. In the yard, which was walled around with stones, he swept the dirt away so that the white marl (caliche) was free of dirt and litter. In his house the floors were polished to a shine. I don't recall what furniture he had in the house, but I do remember the bottles lined up against the wall. I don't know if they were bottles from which he had drunk or if they were bottles he had picked up in his yard, but there was a military precision and cleanliness that baffled us. We couldn't understand how a blind person could have done so many things so very well.

My visits to Mr. Christopher ended abruptly. Every Saturday I would collect a bag of bread from one of the bakers and take it to Mr. Christopher. One Saturday, I did not get the bread from his baker, but from another baker instead. We were neighbors to Minnie and George Ferris and their children, as well as her sister Sarah. We bought bread from Minnie all the time, as well as sugar cakes, peanuts, and everything she sold. I collected the bag of bread from Minnie and headed over to Mr. Christopher. In my zeal and honesty, I told him that I had bought the bread from Minnie. Mr. Christopher got into a rage and informed me that he could not eat Minnie's bread because he remembered seeing yampie, mucus, in her eyes. I was shocked by his behavior. I was also shocked by the words he had uttered. He was blind, and even though he was meticulous in his hygiene, there were times when he had yampie in his eyes. I wondered if he understood what he was saying and if he knew that he was guilty of the thing for which he was rejecting Minnie's bread. I took the bread because he refused to take it. I don't recall what I did with the bag of bread, nor do I know who paid for it. I must have taken it home and had Darling pay for it because I had to explain why I was not returning to his home.

Chapter 22

Attractions and Entertainment

When Aunt Gertie migrated to New York in 1921, she sailed from Antigua to New York. When my sister Ros went to England in 1961, she also sailed from Antigua to England. At that time, the governments of the Caribbean attempted to enhance travelling among the islands. They introduced the *Federal Maple* and the *Federal Palm* that traversed the waters of the Caribbean. Airplanes soon started flying into Antigua and the Coolidge International Airport was constructed to accommodate the planes. Those were the pre-pre-911 days of terrorist activities, and the airport became one of our favorite attractions, and our most popular Sunday afternoon drive.

Local people could not afford to fly, so we did not go to see them off or to welcome their arrival. We were intrigued by the silver birds flying through the sky and landing on our runway. We were very curious to see the people who deplaned. Some were tourists who had reservations at the various hotels, some were businessmen, and others were students returning from boarding schools in their parents' homelands. In those days, there was a green stone wall with a chain-link fence that separated the viewers from the passengers. Additionally, there was a waving gallery upstairs where we would congregate to see who were coming and going. Every Sunday afternoon we would go for a drive and the favorite destination was the Coolidge Airport.

Going for a drive was a metaphor for many things. Only a few people owned cars in Cedar Grove, with my father and Mr. Roseau being two of them. Papa drove an old black car that needed to be cranked to get it started. Once it was started, it would move at the terrific speed of thirty miles per hour. We thought we were speeding. Papa also drove an old pickup truck that we called the Hot Rod. It had a cab and an open bed with no sides and no back. Whenever we rode in the pickup, he would caution us to be careful and sit with our backs against the cab. One day, on our way from Cedar Grove to Powell's Estate, we had just passed Royal Pond and were heading up Santy Hill when P slid off the truck bed and landed on the ground. We were scared to alert Papa because we knew he would have been very angry. We also knew that P was his favorite child, so we thought he would have been lenient with her. We banged on the cab of the truck until he stopped and we told him that P had fallen out. He reversed to the place where we met her walking up the hill. Papa looked as angrily as he could, with one eye looking at P and the other eye wandering off, as it was wont to do. We stayed very quiet, awaiting the explosion that soon came. He said to P, "Get back on the truck. Didn't I tell you to sit close to the cab? I have a good mind to give you a sound beating." With that, he got back into the cab and we drove off to Powell's.

We all felt Sunday was a special day. Many of us in the village went to church, but we performed all other tasks at home. We usually chose not to perform heavy manual labor on that day. Instead, we chose to go to the beach with or without a picnic basket. After a while going to the beach lost that special appeal, and those of us who had access to cars started going for drives on Sundays. We would travel to neighboring or far-off villages to visit friends. Then, when the airport was opened for business, we decided to go to the airport for a drive, which was really just another way of showing off our car and another opportunity to go driving. Sometimes friends would decide to drive with us and we would have a good time. We enjoyed observing the passengers disembark and those who were boarding the plane.

Passengers would dress up. It was not unusual to see men and women in their Sunday best. Travelling was a very new and exciting experience for which we would dress appropriately. We actually got new clothes to travel in. Back then I don't recall there being any limitation on the amount of luggage we were allowed on the flight, so we would be laden down with food and gifts for relatives and acquaintances of acquaintances who lived in the state or country where we were going. It seemed as if many of our acquaintances had no concept of geography. They assumed that anyone

Attractions and Entertainment

going to England must meet others who were in England. They discarded the fact that England was huge and we may not even see or communicate with other Cedar Grovians in England. The same applied for Canada and the United States. They decided to send black fruit cakes, tarts, buns, sugar cakes, guava cheese, peppermint candies, and things they thought couldn't be obtained in New York, Canada, or England. There were also the letters requesting clothing, shoes, and other things that the traveler was supposed to bring back to Antigua. The many gifts that were brought sometimes seemed to take up all the space in the suitcase and the passenger seldom had space for his/her own luggage.

We soon learned that some trips were made without a word spoken to anyone, and the members of the home were told to keep the information in strictest confidence. Economical and time constraints as well as security measures implemented at the airport required us to curtail our visits, so the Sunday drives to the airport soon ceased and we did not often see those who were sneaking out and in without telling a soul.

Chapter 23

Of Parties and Such

We were very hard working people who felt that we should take time for us to recuperate. We seemed to be able to balance our work and leisure to some degree. On holidays like Christmas and New Year's, we kept the home fires burning by cleaning, cooking, and entertaining as only simple folk could. There was always food for those guests who may stop by, as well as for the family. It was amazing that as poor as we were, we were very hospitable. Any home we visited during the holidays would have black fruit cake and sorrel, ginger beer, or maubi. Those were local drinks prepared for the special occasion, but later when bottling plants were established in Antigua, we started stocking up on sweet drinks. The more affluent homes would have the cake and drinks, as well as goat water, cooked ham, and alcohol for the adults.

During Easter, there was not a great emphasis placed on food because neighbors did not visit as they did during Christmas and New Year's. We did go to the beach more frequently. On Good Friday, after we had spent several hours in church going through the Stations of the Cross, we would pack our food and head to Hodges Bay or Boon Point. Even though we planned to luxuriate in the sand, sea, and sun, our primary focus was picking whelks and digging cockles. Those shelled creatures were easily obtainable and did not require us to travel out in a boat or endangering ourselves. The whelks were usually on the rocks and we would pick them off and drop them in our buckets or baskets. We would dig in the sand for the cockle beds and get our fill. They enhanced our meals, adding that special flavor that we all enjoyed. We would cook the whelks until they were done, a skill I have not learned, but our parents knew it and that satisfied us. We would then grab the shell and pull them out and eat them, especially the end filled with their waste matter. The cockle was another matter.

Of Parties and Such

When the cockles were cooked, the white shells would pop open and we would know they were ready. We would take them out of the water that was used to cook the rice. While the rice was being cooked, we would extricate the meat from the shells and put them in a container. We were put under heavy restrictions not to eat any of the cockles because we could easily have eaten all of them and there would be none for the rice. The rice was cooked in the cockle water, which we were told had all the nutrients that our bodies needed. A little before the water dried on the rice, Darling would dump the container of cockles into the rice and start stirring so that they would be evenly distributed. Our mouths would start to water as we anticipated the delicious taste of rice and cockles. Sometimes Darling chose to stew the cockles in a butter sauce that was even more mouthwatering.

Easter Monday was the official picnic day. Schools and churches would plan their picnics on that day, and they would choose to travel to one of the far beaches such as Ffryes Bay at Ffryes Estate, Morris Bay in Old Road, Dark Wood before entering Urlings, Turner's Beach at Cobbs Cross, or Long Bay outside of Willikies. Those long trips required us to sign up and pay a nominal fee for the bus, but we would provide our own picnic lunch that included little fried dumplings, rice and peas with stewed chicken, beef, or goat, salt fish cakes, ducoona with salt fish and provisions, ginger beer, and cake. We would also have sweet biscuits, candies, and assorted nuts. At the beach we would locate a spot under the grape trees and while the adults watched the food, we would jump into the water until it made us hungry enough to get out and eat. Much sharing went on, since we always seemed to like our friends' food more than our own, but they liked ours as well so trading was no problem. We would stay at the beach until the sun began to set and then we would board the buses with all of our belongings and head on home. Most of us were so tired that we would fall asleep on the drive home.

The first Monday in May is celebrated as Labour Day in Antigua. It is the day when the members of the Antigua Trades and Labour Union would get decked out in their red T-shirts and other red apparel and head to Fort James to celebrate the accomplishments of the party that had ruled Antigua for twenty-eight years. The members of the United Progressive Party, the opposition, would head for Ffryes Bay decked out in their royal blue T-shirts and other apparel. They also, would recount their accomplishments and rally the forces to continue their opposition.

The local carnival took place during the summer, which required several days of activities. There were the Queen Show, the Calypso Show, the Prince and Princess Show, the Jaycees Caribbean Queen Show, and other shows, all leading up to the actual Carnival on August Monday, the first Monday in August, which would begin with j'ouvert very early in the morning followed by the parade of floats and troupes later in the day. Tuesday was the last lap when the bands would take to the streets of St. John's. When carnival changed from a cultural activity to vulgar displays of human flesh and the music assumed a raunchy flavor, some of us decided to boycott the activities and go to the beach for a picnic.

Since Antigua gained its independence from Britain in 1981, every November 1 is celebrated as Independence Day. Antiguans around the world would celebrate with various activities such as church services, breakfasts, brunches, dances, and banquets. I supported the activities on St. Croix and considered it my patriotic duty. For the past few years, however, I have chosen to travel to Antigua for that weekend. I was surprised to learn that Antiguans take their Independence very seriously. One year, as I waited on the steps of the Royal Bank of Canada to transact some business on the Friday before Independence, I noticed many people were decked out in the local colors of the madras that were fashioned in unique and creative ways. I heard people greeting each other with, "Happy Independence," and I thought, "These people are really serious about Independence." The following day when I attended church in St. John's, I noticed that both men and women were displaying their national costumes. I must admit that I admired some of the creative fashion designs.

Even though Antigua had been a British colony for more than three centuries and remains connected to the British Empire, Antiguans acknowledge and celebrate American holidays such as Mother's Day, Father's Day, and Thanksgiving Day. They seem to enjoy the best of both worlds.

Chapter 24

Those Glorious Days

I was born in a glorious age in a beautiful country. Although Antigua was a British colony, it provided the forum for its people to articulate their ambitions and to excel at whatever ventures they were interested in. I am extremely grateful to those trailblazers who fought for our rights and forged paths for future generations to live in an independent country. In the 1950s and 1960s, there were distinct differences between town and country, but as the agricultural focus declined, many country people found work in the city, which helped to narrow the gap and eliminate real and imagined differences.

One major reason was the great attraction to the country. Some returning Antiguans were building big houses in the country areas, primarily on hilltops where the view is great. There were no hills in St. John's apart from Scottshill, Michael's Mount, and the hill where Holberton Hospital was located, but those hills were all taken. People started buying lands in the country where they built their homes. That trend has accelerated through the years. Cedar Grovians were migrating in larger numbers and some relocated to other villages in Antigua.

The Cedar Grove of 2013 is only a memory of the Cedar Grove of my birth and youth. Not only have many of us left, but many of our parents have passed away and some of the practices that bound us to the village and to one another have ceased to possess their power. Our places have been filled by expatriates, primarily Jamaicans and Guyanese. Many of the lands we once farmed are now residential areas, boasting huge, unique architectural masterpieces owned by people of all races and origins, people who have no idea of the history of the place or the efforts of those who helped to develop not only the landscape, but the village and the island. The focus seems to have shifted from the neighborly caring village to a pragmatic economical intent, where people seem to be house proud instead of being people centered.

The years of my childhood and youth were glorious years in the annals of Antigua's history. We may not have had the status Antigua now holds in the region and in the world, but we understood the meanings of family, respect, responsibility, and stability. We possessed a work ethic that has helped to mold us into the people we are today. We were interdependent, working with and depending on each other, which justified the truth of the saying, "One hand washes the other." The result was a community sincerely bound together, existing to meet the needs of each other. That factor allowed us to exercise our individuality, while being intricately involved in our community, our village.

The words of Mary Hopkin's popular song of the late 1960s reverberate in my memory, a fitting tribute to the great period and place that produced me:

> *"Those were the days, my friend*
> *I thought they'd never end . . .*
> *Those were the days,*
> *Oh, yes, those were the days!"*

Chapter 25

Some Popular Family Recipes

My mother sold chocolate sticks. She made them from the mound of chocolate that resulted after she had roasted the nuts, shelled, and ground them. We would use the broken sticks or the uncooperative chocolate. We would boil a large pot of water and drop the chocolate in it, leaving it uncovered. After the chocolate dissolved in the hot water we would drop in a cinnamon stick and grate some nutmeg in the liquid. We would then add boiled cow's milk until the mixture was a light brown. Finally, we would sweeten it with brown sugar. Chocolate tea was drunk with Sunday morning breakfast. We varied the chocolate tea by adding white flour, which thickened it, sometimes with little flour lumps. We called that concoction, "stay" and ate it with a spoon usually in the evenings.

Darling's favorite dishes were the ones that went a long way. With thirteen mouths to feed, she attempted to satisfy our hunger while providing the nutrients our bodies required. It was not surprising that our most popular meals were pepper pot, fungi, fried dumplings, boiled dumplings, rice, and soup. They contained a variety of ingredients that stretched the dishes to feed many. We also ate a lot of corned meats and fish.

A typical Antiguan Sunday breakfast required several key ingredients:

- Boiled eggs
- Eggplants, okras, spinach, and green papaya all boiled and chopped together, then sprinkled with black pepper
- Stewed salt fish with much sauce enhanced by tomato paste
- Sliced fried buggaments—short plantains—plantains can be substituted for buggaments
- Chunks of braided ti ti bread
- A large cup of chocolate tea.

There was always enough for everyone and the very brave ones could even have seconds. After we had made our pilgrimages to the churches, we were ready for dinner at about 3:00 or 4:00 p.m. Sunday dinner required advanced preparation. If Darling was going to cook a home grown chicken, she would have one of us catch it, then we would pluck it and turn it over to her. She would clean it by applying lime and vinegar as she washed the bird inside and outside. If she was going to stuff the bird, she would boil the gizzards and the neck. After they were well cooked, she would dice the gizzards into small pieces and extract as much meat as she could from the neck. She would dice the meat and reserve the neck bone for soup or pepperpot. The diced pieces of meat would be included in the stuffing made from stale bread and seasoning.

If she was cooking chicken parts she would cut them up in many pieces, with at least one for each member of the family. My father was always served the biggest and best parts of the meal and he was also served first. Some of us children would linger around until he had eaten because he always left us some morsel that we would gobble up with relish.

A typical Antiguan Sunday dinner included the following dishes:
- Rice and peas—pigeon peas, black eye peas, and any peas that may be available
- Potato salad or baked macaroni and cheese
- Sliced cooked sweet potatoes
- Sliced fried plantains
- Stewed beef, or goat, or chicken; sometimes it may be baked chicken
- Peas and carrots
- Limeade (brebitch)

Desserts weren't usually served. Any food left over from breakfast or dinner was eaten the following day.

Aunt Gertie's meals were more sophisticated and she always served dessert. She always kept ice cream in her "Frigidaire" freezer and she always had a cake, "in case anyone stopped by." One of her favorite desserts was the custard, which is popularly known as flan.

Some Popular Family Recipes

Aunt Gertie's pound cake was special to me because she added a little cornmeal that gave it a special taste and the recipe was easy for me to remember.

Aunt Gertie's Pound Cake:

One lb. of butter
(She liked Anchor butter)
One lb. of white sugar
¾ lb. of flour
¼ lb. of yellow cornmeal
Four eggs

½ cup milk
Two tsps. baking powder
Cinnamon, nutmeg, a dash of salt, and the skin of a lime
¼ tsp. vanilla essence

Sift the dry ingredients together and put them aside. Cream the butter and sugar until it is light and fluffy. Add well beaten eggs, lime skin, and essence and mix them together. Add dry ingredients, alternating with milk. Pour batter in a well-greased pan. Bake at 350°F until the cake is well done when tested.

One of the highlights of our Thursday trip was a visit to Scot's Hill where Aunt Gertie would buy a bag of chicken feet. She would clean them by taking off the skin and cutting the nails before marinating the chicken legs. Early the next morning, she would cook the chicken foot soup.

Aunt Gertie's Chicken Foot Soup

Chicken feet
Sweet potatoes
White potatoes
Tannias
Pumpkin

Flour
Onions, pepper, garlic, thyme, celery
Cooking oil
Salt
Water

In a large container, sauté the chicken feet in the cooking oil with the sliced onions, pepper, garlic, thyme, and celery until they are golden brown. Add a quart of water and let the chicken feet cook on a slow fire.

While that is cooking, peel and dice the sweet potatoes, white potatoes, pumpkin, and tannias. Add them to the partially cooked chicken feet. Let those cook until they are soft. While they are cooking, mix the flour with a dash of salt and some water to make the dumplings. Spoon drop the dumplings or roll them into whatever shape you desire and add them into the boiling pot. Add salt to taste. Turn off the fire. Soup is best when eaten hot.

Glossary of Terms

1. Tapa Hill   Top of the hill
2. La Passa   The pasture
3. Yabba   A large clay dish used for roasting and parching corn, cocoa, peanuts
4. Ashum   An edible powder created by roasting shelled dried corn in a yabba, grinding the roasted corn in a mortar and pestle, then adding brown sugar and nutmeg.
5. Scianze   Proud, arrogant
6. Wagee   Used clothing passed on to others

We invite you to view the complete
selection of titles we publish at:

www.ASPECTBooks.com

Scan with your mobile
device to go directly
to our website.

Please write or email us your praises, reactions, or
thoughts about this or any other book we publish at:

AB ASPECT Books
www.ASPECTBooks.com

P.O. Box 954
Ringgold, GA 30736

info@ASPECTBooks.com

ASPECT Books titles may be purchased in bulk
for educational, business, fund-raising, or sales
promotional use.
For information, please e-mail:

BulkSales@ASPECTBooks.com

Finally, if you are interested in seeing
your own book in print, please contact us at

publishing@ASPECTBooks.com

We would be happy to review your manuscript for free.

www.ingramcontent.com/pod-product-compliance
Lightning Source LLC
Chambersburg PA
CBHW070544170426
43200CB00011B/2545